The Foundations by John Galsworthy

Fourth Series Plays

An Extravagant Play

John Galsworthy was born at Kingston Upon Thames in Surrey, England, on August 14th 1867 to a wealthy and well established family. His schooling was at Harrow and New College, Oxford before training as a barrister and being called to the bar in 1890. However, Law was not attractive to him and he travelled abroad becoming great friends with the novelist Joseph Conrad, then a first mate on a sailing ship.

In 1895 Galsworthy began an affair with Ada Nemesis Pearson Cooper, the wife of his cousin Major Arthur Galsworthy. The affair was kept a secret for 10 years till she at last divorced and they married on 23 September 1905.

John Galsworthy first published in 1897 with a collection of short stories entitled "The Four Winds". For the next 7 years he published these and all works under his pen name John Sinjohn. It was only upon the death of his father and the publication of "The Island Pharisees" in 1904 that he published as John Galsworthy. In this volume we have Villa Rubein ays and studies. They are the work of a supreme talent at the top of his game. Whilst today he is far more well know as a Nobel Prize winning novelist then he was considered a playwright dealing with social issues and the class system. He was appointed to the Order of Merit in 1929, after earlier turning down a knighthood, and awarded the Nobel Prize in 1932 though he was too ill to attend. John Galsworthy died from a brain tumour at his London home, Grove Lodge, Hampstead on January 31st 1933. In accordance with his will he was cremated at Woking with his ashes then being scattered over the South Downs from an aeroplane.

He is now far better known for his novels, particularly The Forsyte Saga, his trilogy about the eponymous family of the same name. These books, as with many of his other works, deal with social class, upper-middle class lives in particular. Although always sympathetic to his characters, he reveals their insular, snobbish, and somewhat greedy attitudes and suffocating moral codes. He is now viewed as one of the first from the Edwardian era to challenge some of the ideals of society depicted in the literature of Victorian England.

In his writings he campaigns for a variety of causes, including prison reform, women's rights, animal welfare, and the opposition of censorship as well as a recurring theme of an unhappy marriage from the women's side. During World War I he worked in a hospital in France as an orderly after being passed over for military service.

He was appointed to the Order of Merit in 1929, after earlier turning down a knighthood, and awarded the Nobel Prize in 1932 though he was too ill to attend.

John Galsworthy died from a brain tumour at his London home, Grove Lodge, Hampstead on January 31st 1933. In accordance with his will he was cremated at Woking with his ashes then being scattered over the South Downs from an aeroplane.

Index of Contents

PERSONS OF THE PLAY
THE SCENE
THE TIME
ACT I
ACT II
ACT III
JOHN GALSWORTHY – A SHORT BIOGRAPHY
JOHN GALSWORTHY – A CONCISE BIBLIOGRAPHY

PERSONS OF THE PLAY

LORD WILLIAM DROMONDY, M.P.
LADY WILLIAM DROMONDY
LITTLE ANNE
MISS STOKES
MR. POULDER
JAMES
HENRY
THOMAS
CHARLES
THE PRESS
LEMMY
OLD MRS. LEMMY
LITTLE AIDA
THE DUKE OF EXETER
Some ANTI-SWEATERS
Some SWEATED WORKERS
A CROWD

THE SCENE

ACT I. The cellar at Lord William Dromondy's in Park Lane.

ACT II. The room of old Mrs Lemmy in Bethnal Green.

ACT III - Ante-room of the hall at Lord William Dromondy's.

THE TIME

The Action passes continuously between 8 and 10.30 of a summer evening, some years after the Great War.

Lord William Dromondy's mansion in Park Lane. Eight o'clock of the evening. **LITTLE ANNE DROMONDY** and the large footman, **JAMES**, gaunt and grin, discovered in the wine cellar, by light of gas. **JAMES**, in plush breeches, is selecting wine.

LITTLE ANNE
James, are you really James?

JAMES
No, my proper name's John.

LITTLE ANNE
Oh! [A pause] And is Charles's an improper name too?

JAMES
His proper name's Mark.

LITTLE ANNE
Then is Thomas Matthew?

JAMES
Miss Anne, stand clear o' that bin. You'll put your foot through one o' those 'ock bottles.

LITTLE ANNE
No, but James—Henry might be Luke, really?

JAMES
Now shut it, Miss Anne!

LITTLE ANNE
Who gave you those names? Not your godfathers and godmothers?

JAMES
Poulder. Butlers think they're the Almighty. [Gloomily] But his name's Bartholomew.

LITTLE ANNE
Bartholomew Poulder? It's rather jolly.

JAMES
It's hidjeous.

LITTLE ANNE
Which do you like to be called—John or James?

JAMES

I don't give a darn.

LITTLE ANNE
What is a darn?

JAMES
'Tain't in the dictionary.

LITTLE ANNE
Do you like my name? Anne Dromondy? It's old, you know. But it's funny, isn't it?

JAMES
[Indifferently] It'll pass.

LITTLE ANNE
How many bottles have you got to pick out?

JAMES
Thirty-four.

LITTLE ANNE
Are they all for the dinner, or for the people who come in to the Anti-Sweating Meeting afterwards?

JAMES
All for the dinner. They give the Sweated—tea.

LITTLE ANNE
All for the dinner? They'll drink too much, won't they?

JAMES
We've got to be on the safe side.

LITTLE ANNE
Will it be safer if they drink too much?

[**JAMES** pauses in the act of dusting a bottle to look at her, as if suspecting irony.

LITTLE ANNE [Sniffing]
Isn't the smell delicious here-like the taste of cherries when they've gone bad—[She sniffs again] and mushrooms; and boot blacking.

JAMES
That's the escape of gas.

LITTLE ANNE
Has the plumber's man been?

JAMES

Yes.

LITTLE ANNE
Which one?

JAMES
Little blighter I've never seen before.

LITTLE ANNE
What is a little blighter? Can I see?

JAMES
He's just gone.

LITTLE ANNE [Straying]
Oh!... James, are these really the foundations?

JAMES
You might 'arf say so. There's a lot under a woppin' big house like this; you can't hardly get to the bottom of it.

LITTLE ANNE
Everything's built on something, isn't it? And what's THAT built on?

JAMES
Ask another.

LITTLE ANNE
If you wanted to blow it up, though, you'd have to begin from here, wouldn't you?

JAMES
Who'd want to blow it up?

LITTLE ANNE
It would make a mess in Park Lane.

JAMES
I've seen a lot bigger messes than this'd make, out in the war.

LITTLE ANNE
Oh! but that's years ago! Was it like this in the trenches, James?

JAMES [Grimly]
Ah! 'Cept that you couldn't lay your 'and on a bottle o' port when you wanted one.

LITTLE ANNE
Do you, when you want it, here?

JAMES [On guard]
I only suggest it's possible.

LITTLE ANNE
Perhaps Poulder does.

JAMES [Icily]
I say nothin' about that.

LITTLE ANNE
Oh! Do say something!

JAMES
I'm ashamed of you, Miss Anne, pumpin' me!

LITTLE ANNE [Reproachfully]
I'm not pumpin'! I only want to make Poulder jump when I ask him.

JAMES [Grinning]
Try it on your own responsibility, then; don't bring me in!

LITTLE ANNE [Switching off]
James, do you think there's going to be a bloody revolution?

JAMES [Shocked]
I shouldn't use that word, at your age.

LITTLE ANNE
Why not? Daddy used it this morning to Mother. [Imitating] "The country's in an awful state, darling; there's going to be a bloody revolution, and we shall all be blown sky-high." Do you like Daddy?

JAMES [Taken aback]
Like Lord William? What do you think? We chaps would ha' done anything for him out there in the war.

LITTLE ANNE
He never says that he always says he'd have done anything for you!

JAMES
Well—that's the same thing.

LITTLE ANNE
It isn't—it's the opposite. What is class hatred, James?

JAMES [Wisely]
Ah! A lot o' people thought when the war was over there'd be no more o' that. [He sniggers] Used to amuse me to read in the papers about the wonderful unity that was comin'. I could ha' told 'em different.

LITTLE ANNE
Why should people hate? I like everybody.

JAMES
You know such a lot o' people, don't you?

LITTLE ANNE
Well, Daddy likes everybody, and Mother likes everybody, except the people who don't like Daddy. I bar Miss Stokes, of course; but then, who wouldn't?

JAMES [With a touch of philosophy]
That's right—we all bars them that tries to get something out of us.

LITTLE ANNE
Who do you bar, James?

JAMES
Well—[Enjoying the luxury of thought]—Speaking generally, I bar everybody that looks down their noses at me. Out there in the trenches, there'd come a shell, and orf'd go some orficer's head, an' I'd think: That might ha' been me—we're all equal in the sight o' the stars. But when I got home again among the torfs, I says to meself: Out there, ye know, you filled a hole as well as me; but here you've put it on again, with mufti.

LITTLE ANNE
James, are your breeches made of mufti?

JAMES [Contemplating his legs with a certain contempt]
Ah! Footmen were to ha' been off; but Lord William was scared we wouldn't get jobs in the rush. We're on his conscience, and it's on my conscience that I've been on his long enough—so, now I've saved a bit, I'm goin' to take meself orf it.

LITTLE ANNE
Oh! Are you going? Where?

JAMES [Assembling the last bottles]
Out o' Blighty!

LITTLE ANNE
Is a little blighter a little Englishman?

JAMES [Embarrassed]
Well-'e can be.

LITTLE ANNE [Mining]
James—we're quite safe down here, aren't we, in a revolution? Only, we wouldn't have fun. Which would you rather—be safe, or have fun?

JAMES [Grimly]

Well, I had my bit o' fun in the war.

LITTLE ANNE
I like fun that happens when you're not looking.

JAMES
Do you? You'd ha' been just suited.

LITTLE ANNE
James, is there a future life? Miss Stokes says so.

JAMES
It's a belief, in the middle classes.

LITTLE ANNE
What are the middle classes?

JAMES
Anything from two 'undred a year to supertax.

LITTLE ANNE
Mother says they're terrible. Is Miss Stokes middle class?

JAMES
Yes.

LITTLE ANNE
Then I expect they are terrible. She's awfully virtuous, though, isn't she?

JAMES
'Tisn't so much the bein' virtuous, as the lookin' it, that's awful.

LITTLE ANNE
Are all the middle classes virtuous? Is Poulder?

JAMES [Dubiously]
Well. Ask him!

LITTLE ANNE
Yes, I will. Look!

[From an empty bin on the ground level she picks up a lighted taper,—burnt almost to the end.

JAMES [Contemplating it]
Careless!

LITTLE ANNIE
Oh! And look!

[She paints to a rounded metal object lying in the bin, close to where the taper was.

It's a bomb!

[She is about to pick it up when **JAMES** takes her by the waist and puts her aside.

JAMES [Sternly]
You stand back, there! I don't like the look o' that!

LITTLE ANNE [With intense interest]
Is it really a bomb? What fun!

JAMES
Go and fetch Poulder while I keep an eye on it.

LITTLE ANNE [On tiptoe of excitement]
If only I can make him jump! Oh, James! we needn't put the light out, need we?

JAMES
No. Clear off and get him, and don't you come back.

LITTLE ANNE
Oh! but I must! I found it!

JAMES
Cut along.

LITTLE ANNE
Shall we bring a bucket?

JAMES
Yes.

[**LITTLE ANNE** flies off.

JAMES [Gazing at the object]
Near go! Thought I'd seen enough o'them to last my time. That little gas blighter! He looked a rum 'un, too—one o' these 'ere Bolshies.

[In the presence of this grim object the habits of the past are too much for him. He sits on the ground, leaning against one of the bottle baskets, keeping his eyes on the bomb, his large, lean, gorgeous body spread, one elbow on his plush knee. Taking out an empty pipe, he places it mechanically, bowl down, between his dips. There enter, behind him, as from a communication trench, **POULDER**, in swallow-tails, with **LITTLE ANNE** behind him.

LITTLE ANNE [Peering round him—ecstatic]
Hurrah! Not gone off yet! It can't—can it—while James is sitting on it?

POULDER [Very broad and stout, with square shoulders,—a large ruddy face, and a small mouth]
No noise, Miss.—James.

JAMES
Hallo!

POULDER
What's all this?

JAMES
Bomb!

POULDER
Miss Anne, off you go, and don't you—

LITTLE ANNE
Come back again! I know!

[She flies.

JAMES [Extending his hand with the pipe in it]
See!

POULDER [Severely]
You've been at it again! Look here, you're not in the trenches now. Get up! What are your breeches goin' to be like? You might break a bottle any moment!

JAMES [Rising with a jerk to a sort of "Attention!"]
Look here, you starched antiquity, you and I and that bomb are here in the sight of the stars. If you don't look out I'll stamp on it and blow us all to glory! Drop your civilian swank!

POULDER [Seeing red]
Ho! Because you had the privilege of fightin' for your country you still think you can put it on, do you? Take up your wine! 'Pon my word, you fellers have got no nerve left!

[**JAMES** makes a sudden swoop, lifts the bomb and poises it in both hands. **POULDER** recoils against a bin and gazes, at the object.

JAMES
Put up your hands!

POULDER
I defy you to make me ridiculous.

JAMES [Fiercely]
Up with 'em!

[**POULDER'S** hands go up in an uncontrollable spasm, which he subdues almost instantly, pulling them down again.

JAMES
Very good.

[He lowers the bomb.

POULDER [Surprised]
I never lifted 'em.

JAMES
You'd have made a first-class Boche, Poulder. Take the bomb yourself; you're in charge of this section.

POULDER [Pouting]
It's no part of my duty to carry menial objects; if you're afraid of it I'll send 'Enry.

JAMES
Afraid! You 'Op o' me thumb!

[From the "communication trench" appears **LITTLE ANNE**, followed by a thin, sharp, sallow-faced man of thirty-five or so, and another **FOOTMAN**, carrying a wine-cooler.

LITTLE ANNE
I've brought the bucket, and the Press.

PRESS [In front of **POULDER'S** round eyes and mouth]
Ah, major domo, I was just taking the names of the Anti-Sweating dinner.

[He catches sight of the bomb in **JAMES'S** hand.

By George! What A.1. irony!

[He brings out a note-book and writes.

"Highest class dining to relieve distress of lowest class-bombed by same!" Tipping!

[He rubs his hands.

POULDER [Drawing himself up]
Sir? This is present!

[He indicates **LITTLE ANNE** with the flat of his hand.

LITTLE ANNE
I found the bomb.

PRESS [Absorbed]

By Jove! This is a piece of luck!

[He writes.

POULDER [Observing him]
This won't do—it won't do at all!

PRESS [Writing-absorbed]
"Beginning of the British Revolution!"

POULDER [To **JAMES**]
Put it in the cooler. 'Enry, 'old up the cooler. Gently! Miss Anne, get be'ind the Press.

JAMES [Grimly—holding the bomb above the cooler]
It won't be the Press that'll stop Miss Anne's goin' to 'Eaven if one o' this sort goes off. Look out! I'm goin' to drop it.

[**ALL** recoil. **HENRY** puts the cooler down and backs away.

LITTLE ANNE [Dancing forward]
Oh! Let me see! I missed all the war, you know!

[**JAMES** lowers the bomb into the cooler.

POULDER [Regaining courage—to **THE PRESS**, who is scribbling in his note-book]
If you mention this before the police lay their hands on it, it'll be contempt o' Court.

PRESS [Struck]
I say, major domo, don't call in the police! That's the last resort. Let me do the Sherlocking for you. Who's been down here?

LITTLE ANNE
The plumber's man about the gas—a little blighter we'd never seen before.

JAMES
Lives close by, in Royal Court Mews—No. 3. I had a word with him before he came down. Lemmy his name is.

PRESS
"Lemmy!" [Noting the address] Right-o!

LITTLE ANNE
Oh! Do let me come with you!

POULDER [Barring the way]
I've got to lay it all before Lord William.

PRESS

Ah! What's he like?

POULDER [With dignity]
A gentleman, sir.

PRESS
Then he won't want the police in.

POULDER
Nor the Press, if I may go so far, as to say so.

PRESS
One to you! But I defy you to keep this from the Press, major domo: This is the most significant thing that has happened in our time. Guy Fawkes is nothing to it. The foundations of Society reeling! By George, it's a second Bethlehem!

[He writes.

POULDER [To **JAMES**]
Take up your wine and follow me. 'Enry, bring the cooler. Miss Anne, precede us. [To **THE PRESS**] You defy me? Very well; I'm goin' to lock you up here.

PRESS [Uneasy]
I say this is medieval.

[He attempts to pass.

POULDER [Barring the way]
Not so! James, put him up in that empty 'ock bin. We can't have dinner disturbed in any way.

JAMES [Putting his hands on **THE PRESS'S** shoulders]
Look here—go quiet! I've had a grudge against you yellow newspaper boys ever since the war—frothin' up your daily hate, an' makin' the Huns desperate. You nearly took my life five hundred times out there. If you squeal, I'm gain' to take yours once—and that'll be enough.

PRESS
That's awfully unjust. Im not yellow!

JAMES
Well, you look it. Hup.

PRESS
Little Lady-Anne, haven't you any authority with these fellows?

LITTLE ANNE [Resisting **POULDER'S** pressure]
I won't go! I simply must see James put him up!

PRESS

Now, I warn you all plainly—there'll be a leader on this.

[He tries to bolt but is seized by **JAMES**.

JAMES [Ironically]
Ho!

PRESS
My paper has the biggest influence

JAMES
That's the one! Git up in that 'ock bin, and mind your feet among the claret.

PRESS
This is an outrage on the Press.

JAMES
Then it'll wipe out one by the Press on the Public—an' leave just a million over! Hup!

POULDER
'Enry, give 'im an 'and.

[**THE PRESS** mounts, assisted by **JAMES** and **HENRY**.

LITTLE ANNE [Ecstatic]
It's lovely!

POULDER [Nervously]
Mind the '87! Mind!

JAMES
Mind your feet in Mr. Poulder's favourite wine!

[A **WOMAN'S** voice is heard, as from the depths of a cave, calling "Anne! Anne!"

LITTLE ANNE [Aghast]
Miss Stokes—I must hide!

[She gets behind **POULDER**. The three **SERVANTS** achieve dignified positions in front of the bins. The voice comes nearer. **THE PRESS** sits dangling his feet, grinning. **MISS STOKES** appears. She is woman of forty-five and terribly good manners. Her greyish hair is rolled back off her forehead. She is in a high evening dress, and in the dim light radiates a startled composure.

MISS STOKES
Poulder, where is Miss Anne?

[**LITTLE ANNE** lays hold of the backs of his legs.

POULDER [Wincing]
I am not in a position to inform you, Miss.

MISS STOKES
They told me she was down here. And what is all this about a bomb?

POULDER [Lifting his hand in a calming manner]
The crisis is past; we have it in ice, Miss. 'Enry, show Miss Stokes!

[**HENRY** indicates the cooler.

MISS STOKES
Good gracious! Does Lord William know?

POULDER
Not at present, Miss.

MISS STOKES
But he ought to, at once.

POULDER
We 'ave 'ad complications.

MISS STOKES [Catching sight of the legs of **THE PRESS**]
Dear me! What are those?

JAMES [Gloomily]
The complications.

[**MISS STOKES** pins up her glasses and stares at them.

PRESS [Cheerfully]
Miss Stokes, would you kindly tell Lord William I'm here from the Press, and would like to speak to him?

MISS STOKES
But—er—why are you up there?

JAMES
'E got up out o' remorse, Miss.

MISS STOKES
What do you mean, James?

PRESS [Warmly]
Miss Stokes, I appeal to you. Is it fair to attribute responsibility to an unsigned journalist—for what he has to say?

JAMES [Sepulchrally]

Yes, when you've got 'im in a nice dark place.

MISS STOKES
James, be more respectful! We owe the Press a very great debt.

JAMES
I'm goin' to pay it, Miss.

MISS STOKES [At a loss]
Poulder, this is really most—

POULDER
I'm bound to keep the Press out of temptation, miss, till I've laid it all before Lord William. 'Enry, take up the cooler. James, watch 'im till we get clear, then bring on the rest of the wine and lock up. Now, Miss.

MISS STOKES
But where is Anne?

PRESS
Miss Stokes, as a lady—!

MISS STOKES
I shall go and fetch Lord William!

POULDER
We will all go, Miss.

LITTLE ANNE [Rushing out from behind his legs]
No—me!

[She eludes **MISS STOKES** and vanishes, followed by that distracted but still well-mannered lady.

POULDER [Looking at his watch]
'Enry, leave the cooler, and take up the wine; tell Thomas to lay it out; get the champagne into ice, and 'ave Charles 'andy in the 'all in case some literary bounder comes punctual.

[**HENRY** takes up the wine and goes.

PRESS [Above his head]
I say, let me down. This is a bit undignified, you know. My paper's a great organ.

POULDER [After a moment's hesitation]
Well—take 'im down, James; he'll do some mischief among the bottles.

JAMES
'Op off your base, and trust to me.

[**THE PRESS** slides off the bin's edge, is received by **JAMES**, and not landed gently.

POULDER [Contemplating him]
The incident's closed; no ill-feeling, I hope?

PRESS
No-o.

POULDER
That's right. [Clearing his throat] While we're waitin' for Lord William—if you're interested in wine—[Philosophically] you can read the history of the times in this cellar. Take 'ock: [He points to a bin] Not a bottle gone. German product, of course. Now, that 'ock is 'sa 'avin' the time of its life—maturin' grandly; got a wonderful chance. About the time we're bringin' ourselves to drink it, we shall be havin' the next great war. With luck that 'ock may lie there another quarter of a century, and a sweet pretty wine it'll be. I only hope I may be here to drink it. Ah! [He shakes his head]—but look at claret! Times are hard on claret. We're givin' it an awful doin'. Now, there's a Ponty Canny [He points to a bin] if we weren't so 'opelessly allied with France, that wine would have a reasonable future. As it is—none! We drink it up and up; not more than sixty dozen left. And where's its equal to come from for a dinner wine—ah! I ask you? On the other hand, port is steady; made in a little country, all but the cobwebs and the old boot flavour; guaranteed by the British Nary; we may 'ope for the best with port. Do you drink it?

PRESS
When I get the chance.

POULDER
Ah! [Clears his throat] I've often wanted to ask: What do they pay you—if it's not indelicate?

[**THE PRESS** shrugs his shoulders.

Can you do it at the money?

[**THE PRESS** shakes his head.

Still—it's an easy life! I've regretted sometimes that I didn't have a shot at it myself; influencin' other people without disclosin' your identity—something very attractive about that. [Lowering his voice] Between man and man, now-what do you think of the situation of the country—these processions of the unemployed—the Red Flag an' the Marsillaisy in the streets—all this talk about an upheaval?

PRESS
Well, speaking as a Socialist—

POULDER [Astounded]
Why; I thought your paper was Tory!

PRESS
So it is. That's nothing!

POULDER [Open-mouthed]
Dear me! [Pointing to the bomb] Do you really think there's something in this?

JAMES [Sepulchrally]
'Igh explosive.

PRESS [Taking out his note-book]
Too much, anyway, to let it drop.

[A pleasant voice calls "Poulder! Hallo!".

POULDER [Forming a trumpet with his hand]
Me Lord!

[As **LORD WILLIAM** appears, **JAMES**, overcome by reminiscences; salutes, and is mechanically answered. **LORD WILLIAM** has "charm." His hair and moustache are crisp and just beginning to grizzle. His bearing is free, easy, and only faintly armoured. He will go far to meet you any day. He is in full evening dress.]

LORD WILLIAM
[Cheerfully] I say, Poulder, what have you and James been doing to the Press? Liberty of the Press—it isn't what it was, but there is a limit. Where is he?

[He turns to **JAMES** between whom and himself there is still the freemasonry of the trenches.]

JAMES [Pointing to **POULDER**]
Be'ind the parapet, me Lord.

[**THE PRESS** mopes out from where he has involuntarily been. screened by **POULDER**, who looks at **JAMES** severely. **LORD WILLIAM** hides a smile.

PRESS
Very glad to meet you, Lord William. My presence down here is quite involuntary.

LORD WILLIAM
[With a charming smile] I know. The Press has to put its—er—to go to the bottom of everything. Where's this bomb, Poulder? Ah!

[He looks into the wine cooler.

PRESS
[Taking out his note-book] Could I have a word with you on the crisis, before dinner, Lord William?

LORD WILLIAM
It's time you and James were up, Poulder. [Indicating the cooler] Look after this; tell Lady William I'll be there in a minute.

POULDER
Very good, me Lord.

[He goes, followed by **JAMES** carrying the cooler.

[As **THE PRESS** turns to look after them, **LORD WILLIAM** catches sight of his back.]

LORD WILLIAM
I must apologise, sir. Can I brush you?

PRESS
[Dusting himself] Thanks; it's only behind. [He opens his note-book] Now, Lord William, if you'd kindly outline your views on the national situation; after such a narrow escape from death, I feel they might have a moral effect. My paper, as you know, is concerned with—the deeper aspect of things. By the way, what do you value your house and collection at?

LORD WILLIAM [Twisting his little mustache]
Really: I can't! Really!

PRESS
Might I say a quarter of a million-lifted in two seconds and a half-hundred thousand to the second. It brings it home, you know.

LORD WILLIAM
No, no; dash it! No!

PRESS [Disappointed]
I see—not draw attention to your property in the present excited state of public feeling? Well, suppose we approach it from the viewpoint of the Anti-Sweating dinner. I have the list of guests—very weighty!

LORD WILLIAM
Taken some lifting-wouldn't they?

PRESS [Seriously]
May I say that you designed the dinner to soften the tension, at this crisis? You saw that case, I suppose, this morning, of the woman dying of starvation in Bethnal Green?

LORD WILLIAM [Desperately]
Yes-yes! I've been horribly affected. I always knew this slump would come after the war, sooner or later.

PRESS [Writing]
"... had predicted slump."

LORD WILLIAM
You see, I've been an Anti-Sweating man for years, and I thought if only we could come together now....

PRESS [Nodding]
I see—I see! Get Society interested in the Sweated, through the dinner. I have the menu here.

[He produces it.

LORD WILLIAM
Good God, man—more than that! I want to show the people that we stand side by side with them, as we did in the trenches. The whole thing's too jolly awful. I lie awake over it.

[He walks up and down.

PRESS [Scribbling]
One moment, please. I'll just get that down—"Too jolly awful—lies awake over it. Was wearing a white waistcoat with pearl buttons." [At a sign of resentment from his victim.] I want the human touch, Lord William—it's everything in my paper. What do you say about this attempt to bomb you?

LORD WILLIAM
Well, in a way I think it's d—d natural

PRESS [Scribbling]
"Lord William thought it d—d natural."

LORD WILLIAM [Overhearing]
No, no; don't put that down. What I mean is, I should like to get hold of those fellows that are singing the Marseillaise about the streets—fellows that have been in the war—real sports they are, you know—thorough good chaps at bottom—and say to them: "Have a feeling heart, boys; put yourself in my position." I don't believe a bit they'd want to bomb me then.

[He walks up and down.

PRESS [Scribbling and muttering "The idea, of brotherhood—" D'you mind my saying that? Word brotherhood—always effective—always—

[He writes.

LORD WILLIAM [Bewildered]
"Brotherhood!" Well, it's pure accident that I'm here and they're there. All the same, I can't pretend to be starving. Can't go out into Hyde Park and stand on a tub, can I? But if I could only show them what I feel—they're such good chaps—poor devils.

PRESS
I quite appreciate! [He writes] "Camel and needle's eye." You were at Eton and Oxford? Your constituency I know. Clubs? But I can get all that. Is it your view that Christianity is on the up-grade, Lord William?

LORD WILLIAM [Dubious]
What d'you mean by Christianity—loving—kindness and that? Of course I think that dogma's got the knock.

[He walks.

PRESS [Writing]

"Lord William thought dogma had got the knock." I should like you just to develop your definition of Christianity. "Loving—kindness" strikes rather a new note.

LORD WILLIAM
New? What about the Sermon on the Mount?

PRESS [Writing]
"Refers to Sermon on Mount." I take it you don't belong to any Church, Lord William?

LORD WILLIAM [Exasperated]
Well, really—I've been baptised and that sort of thing. But look here—

PRESS
Oh! you can trust me—I shan't say anything that you'll regret. Now, do you consider that a religious revival would help to quiet the country?

LORD WILLIAM
Well, I think it would be a deuced, good thing if everybody were a bit more kind.

PRESS
Ah! [Musing] I feel that your views are strikingly original, Lord William. If you could just open out on them a little more? How far would you apply kindness in practice?

LORD WILLIAM
Can you apply it in theory?

PRESS
I believe it is done. But would you allow yourself to be blown up with impunity?

LORD WILLIAM
Well, that's a bit extreme. But I quite sympathise with this chap. Imagine yourself in his shoes. He sees a huge house, all these bottles; us swilling them down; perhaps he's got a starving wife, or consumptive kids.

PRESS [Writing and murmuring]
Um-m! "Kids."

LORD WILLIAM
He thinks: "But for the grace of God, there swill I. Why should that blighter have everything and I nothing?" and all that.

PRESS [Writing]
"And all that." [Eagerly] Yes?

LORD WILLIAM
And gradually—you see—this contrast—becomes an obsession with him. "There's got to be an example made," he thinks; and—er—he makes it, don't you know?

PRESS [Writing]

Ye-es? And—when you're the example?

LORD WILLIAM

Well, you feel a bit blue, of course. But my point is that you quite see it.

PRESS

From the other world. Do you believe in a future life, Lord William? The public took a lot of interest in the question, If you remember, at the time of the war. It might revive at any moment, if there's to be a revolution.

LORD WILLIAM

The wish is always father to the thought, isn't it?

PRESS

Yes! But—er—doesn't the question of a future life rather bear on your point about kindness? If there isn't one—why be kind?

LORD WILLIAM

Well, I should say one oughtn't to be kind for any motive—that's self-interest; but just because one feels it, don't you know.

PRESS [Writing vigorously]

That's very new—very new!

LORD WILLIAM [Simply]

You chaps are wonderful.

PRESS [Doubtfully]

You mean we're—we're—

LORD WILLIAM

No, really. You have such a d—d hard time. It must be perfectly beastly to interview fellows like me.

PRESS

Oh! Not at all, Lord William. Not at all. I assure you compared with a literary man, it's—it's almost heavenly.

LORD WILLIAM

You must have a wonderful knowledge of things.

PRESS [Bridling a little]

Well—I shouldn't say that.

LORD WILLIAM

I don't see how you can avoid it. You turn your hands to everything.

PRESS [Modestly]

Well—yes, Yes.

LORD WILLIAM
I say: Is there really going to be a revolution, or are you making it up, you Press?

PRESS
We don't know. We never know whether we come before the event, or it comes before us.

LORD WILLIAM
That's—very deep—very dip. D'you mind lending me your note-book a moment. I'd like to stick that down. All right, I'll use the other end.

[**THE PRESS** hands it hypnotically.

LORD WILLIAM [Jotting]
Thanks awfully. Now what's your real opinion of the situation?

PRESS
As a man or a Press man?

LORD WILLIAM
Is there any difference?

PRESS
Is there any connection?

LORD WILLIAM
Well, as a man.

PRESS
As a man, I think it's rotten.

LORD WILLIAM
[Jotting] "Rotten." And as a pressman?

PRESS [Smiling]
Prime.

LORD WILLIAM
What! Like a Stilton cheese. Ha, ha!

[He is about to write.

PRESS
My stunt, Lord William. You said that.

[He jots it on his cuff.

LORD WILLIAM

But look here! Would you say that a strong press movement would help to quiet the country?

PRESS

Well, as you ask me, Lord William, I'll tell you. No newspapers for a month would do the trick.

LORD WILLIAM

[Jotting] By Jove! That's brilliant.

PRESS

Yes, but I should starve.

[He suddenly looks up, and his eyes, like gimlets, bore their way into **LORD WILLIAM'S** pleasant, troubled face.

Lord William, you could do me a real kindness. Authorise me to go and interview the fellow who left the bomb here; I've got his address. I promise you to do it most discreetly. Fact is—well—I'm in low water. Since the war we simply can't get sensation enough for the new taste. Now, if I could have an article headed: "Bombed and Bomber"—sort of double interview, you know, it'd very likely set me on my legs again. [Very earnestly] Look!

[He holds out his frayed wristbands.

LORD WILLIAM [Grasping his hand]

My dear chap, certainly. Go and interview this blighter, and then bring him round here. You can do that for one. I'd very much like to see him, as a matter of fact.

PRESS

Thanks awfully; I shall never forget it. Oh! might I have my note-book?

[**LORD WILLIAM** hands it back.

LORD WILLIAM

And look here, if there's anything—when a fellow's fortunate and another's not—

[He puts his hand into his breast pocket.]

PRESS

Oh, thank you! But you see, I shall have to write you up a bit, Lord William. The old aristocracy—you know what the public still expects; if you were to lend me money, you might feel—

LORD WILLIAM

By Jove! Never should have dreamt—

PRESS

No! But it wouldn't do. Have you a photograph of yourself.

LORD WILLIAM

Not on me.

PRESS
Pity! By the way, has it occurred to you that there may be another bomb on the premises?

LORD WILLIAM
Phew! I'll have a look.

[He looks at his watch, and begins hurriedly searching the bins, bending down and going on his knees.
THE PRESS reverses the notebook again and sketches him.

PRESS [To himself]
Ah! That'll do. "Lord William examines the foundations of his house."

[A voice calls "Bill!" **THE PRESS** snaps the note-book to, and looks up. There, where the "communication trench" runs in, stands a tall and elegant woman in the extreme of evening dress.

[With presence of mind] Lady William? You'll find Lord William—Oh! Have you a photograph of him?

LADY WILLIAM
Not on me.

PRESS [Eyeing her]
Er—no—I suppose not—no. Excuse me!

[He sidles past her and is gone.

LADY WILLIAM [With lifted eyebrows]
Bill!

LORD WILLIAM [Emerging, dusting his knees]
Hallo, Nell! I was just making sure there wasn't another bomb.

LADY WILLIAM
Yes; that's why I came dawn: Who was that person?

LORD WILLIAM
Press.

LADY WILLIAM
He looked awfully yellow. I hope you haven't been giving yourself away.

LORD WILLIAM [Dubiously]
Well, I don't know. They're like corkscrews.

LADY WILLIAM
What did he ask you?

LORD WILLIAM
What didn't he?

LADY WILLIAM
Well, what did you tell him?

LORD WILLIAM
That I'd been baptised—but he promised not to put it down.

LADY WILLIAM
Bill, you are absurd.

[She gives a light Little laugh.

LORD WILLIAM
I don't remember anything else, except that it was quite natural we should be bombed, don't you know.

LADY WILLIAM
Why, what harm have we done?

LORD WILLIAM
Been born, my dear. [Suddenly serious] I say, Nell, how am I to tell what this fellow felt when he left that bomb here?

LADY WILLIAM
Why do you want to?

LORD WILLIAM
Out there one used to know what one's men felt.

LADY WILLIAM [Staring]
My dear boy, I really don't think you ought to see the Press; it always upsets you.

LORD WILLIAM
Well! Why should you and I be going to eat ourselves silly to improve the condition of the sweated, when—

LADY WILLIAM [Calmly]
When they're going to "improve" ours, if we don't look out. We've got to get in first, Bill.

LORD WILLIAM [Gloomily]
I know. It's all fear. That's it! Here we are, and here we shall stay—as if there'd never been a war.

LADY WILLIAM
Well, thank heaven there's no "front" to a revolution. You and I can go to glory together this time. Compact! Anything that's on, I'm to abate in.

LORD WILLIAM

Well, in reason.

LADY WILLIAM
No, in rhyme, too.

LORD WILLIAM
I say, your dress!

LADY WILLIAM
Yes, Poulder tried to stop me, but I wasn't going to have you blown up without me.

LORD WILLIAM
You duck. You do look stunning. Give us a kiss!

LADY WILLIAM [Starting back]
Oh, Bill! Don't touch me—your hands!

LORD WILLIAM
Never mind, my mouth's clean.

They stand about a yard apart, and banding their faces towards each other, kiss on the lips.

LITTLE ANNE [Appearing suddenly from the "communication trench," and tip-toeing silently between them]
Oh, Mum! You and Daddy ARE wasting time! Dinner's ready, you know!

CURTAIN

ACT II

The single room of old **MRS LEMMY**, in a small grey house in Bethnal Green, the room of one cumbered by little save age, and the crockery debris of the past. A bed, a cupboard, a coloured portrait of Queen Victoria, and—of all things—a fiddle, hanging on the wall. By the side of old **MRS LEMMY** in her chair is a pile of corduroy trousers, her day's sweated sewing, and a small table. She sits with her back to the window, through which, in the last of the light, the opposite side of the little grey street is visible under the evening sky, where hangs one white cloud shaped like a horned beast. She is still sewing, and her lips move. Being old, and lonely, she has that habit of talking to herself, distressing to those who cannot overhear. From the smack of her tongue she was once a West Country cottage woman; from the look of her creased, parchment face, she was once a pretty girl with black eyes, in which there is still much vitality. The door is opened with difficulty and a little girl enters, carrying a pile of unfinished corduroy trousers nearly as large as herself. She puts them down against the wall, and advances. She is eleven or twelve years old; large-eyed, dark haired, and sallow. Half a woman of this and half of another world, except when as now, she is as irresponsible a bit of life as a little flowering weed growing out of a wall. She stands looking at **MRS LEMMY** with dancing eyes.

LITTLE AIDA

I've brought yer to-morrer's trahsers. Y'nt yer finished wiv to-dy's? I want to tyke 'em.

MRS LEMMY
No, me dear. Drat this last one—me old fengers!

LITTLE AIDA
I learnt some poytry to-dy—I did.

MRS LEMMY
Well, I never!

LITTLE AIDA [Reciting with unction]
"Little lamb who myde thee?
Dost thou know who myde thee,
Gyve thee life and byde thee feed
By the stream and oer the mead;
Gyve the clothing of delight,
Softest clothing, woolly, bright;
Gyve thee such a tender voice,
Myking all the vyles rejoice.
Little lamb who myde thee?
Dost thou know who myde thee?"

MRS LEMMY
'Tes wonderful what things they tache ya nowadays.

LITTLE AIDA
When I grow up I'm goin' to 'ave a revolver an' shoot the people that steals my jools.

MRS LEMMY
Deary-me, wherever du yu get yore notions?

LITTLE AIDA
An' I'm goin' to ride on as 'orse be'ind a man; an' I'm goin' to ryce trynes in my motor car.

MRS LEMMY [Dryly]
Ah!—Yu'um gwine to be very busy, that's sartin. Can you sew?

LITTLE AIDA [With a Smile]
Nao.

MRS LEMMY
Don' they tache Yu that, there?

LITTLE AIDA [Blending contempt and a lingering curiosity]
Nao.

MRS LEMMY

'Tes wonderful genteel.

LITTLE AIDA
I can sing, though.

MRS LEMMY
Let's 'ear yu, then.

LITTLE AIDA [Shaking her head]
I can ply the pianner. I can ply a tune.

MRS LEMMY
Whose pianner?

LITTLE AIDA
Mrs. Brahn's when she's gone aht.

MRS LEMMY
Well, yu are gettin' edjucation! Du they tache yu to love yore neighbours?

LITTLE AIDA [Ineffably]
Nao. [Straying to the window] Mrs. Lemmy, what's the moon?

MRS LEMMY
The mune? Us used to zay 'twas made o' crame cheese.

LITTLE AIDA
I can see it.

MRS LEMMY
Ah! Don' yu never go wishin' for it, me dear.

LITTLE AIDA
I daon't.

MRS LEMMY
Folks as wish for the mune never du no gude.

LITTLE AIDA [Craning out, brilliant]
I'm goin' dahn in the street. I'll come back for yer trahsers.

MRS LEMMY
Well; go yu, then, and get a breath o' fresh air in yore chakes. I'll sune 'a feneshed.

LITTLE AIDA [Solemnly]
I'm goin' to be a dancer, I am.

[She rushes suddenly to the door, pulls it open, and is gone.

MRS LEMMY [Looking after her, and talking to herself.]

Ah! 'Er've a-got all 'er troubles before 'er! "Little lamb, a made'ee?" [Cackling] 'Tes a funny world, tu! [She sings to herself.]

"There is a green 'ill far away
Without a city wall,
Where our dear-Lord was crucified,
'U died to save us all."

[The door is opened, and **LEMMY** comes in; a little man with a stubble of dark moustache and spiky dark hair; large, peculiar eyes he has, and a look of laying his ears back, a look of doubting, of perversity with laughter up the sleeve, that grows on those who have to do with gas and water. He shuts the door.

MRS LEMMY

Well, Bob, I 'aven't a-seen yu this tu weeks.

[**LEMMY** comes up to his mother, and sits down on a stool, sets a tool-bag between his knees, and speaks in a cockney voice.

LEMMY

Well, old lydy o' leisure! Wot would y' 'ave for supper, if yer could choose—salmon wivaht the tin, an' tipsy cyke?

MRS LEMMY [Shaking her head and smiling blandly]

That's showy. Toad in the 'ole I'd 'ave—and a glass o' port wine.

LEMMY

Providential.

[He opens a tool-bag.

Wot dyer think I've got yer?

MRS LEMMY

I 'ope yu've a-got yureself a job, my son!

LEMMY [With his peculiar smile]

Yus, or I couldn't 'ave afforded yer this.

[He takes out a bottle.

Not 'arf! This'll put the blood into yer. Pork wine—once in the cellars of the gryte. We'll drink the ryyal family in this.

[He apostrophises the portrait of Queen Victoria.

MRS LEMMY

Ah! She was a praaper gude queen. I see 'er once, when 'er was bein' burried.

LEMMY

Ryalties—I got nothin' to sy agynst 'em in this country. But the STYTE 'as got to 'ave its pipes seen to. The 'ole show's goin' up pop. Yer'll wyke up one o' these dyes, old lydy, and find yerself on the roof, wiv nuffin' between yer an' the grahnd.

MRS LEMMY

I can't tell what yu'm talkin' about.

LEMMY

We're goin' to 'ave a triumpherat in this country Liberty, Equality, Fraternity; an' if yer arsk me, they won't be in power six months before they've cut each other's throats. But I don't care—I want to see the blood flow! (Dispassionately) I don' care 'oose blood it is. I want to see it flow!

MRS LEMMY [Indulgently]

Yu'm a funny boy, that's sartin.

LEMMY [Carving at the cork with a knife]

This 'ere cork is like Sasiety—rotten; it's old—old an' moulderin'. [He holds up a bit of cork on the point of the knife] Crumblin' under the wax, it is. In goes the screw an' out comes the cork. [With unction]—an' the blood flows.

[Tipping the bottle, he lets a drop fall into the middle of his hand, and licks it up. Gazing with queer and doubting commiseration at has mother.

LEMMY

Well, old dear, wot shall we 'ave it aht of—the gold loving-cup, or—what? 'Ave yer supper fust, though, or it'll go to yer 'ead!

[He goes to the cupboard and taken out a disk in which a little bread is sopped in a little' milk.

LEMMY

Cold pap! 'Ow can yer? 'Yn't yer got a kipper in the 'ouse?

MRS LEMMY [Admiring the bottle]

Port wine! 'Tis a brave treat! I'll 'ave it out of the "Present from Margitt," Bob. I tuk 'ee therr by excursion when yu was six months. Yu 'ad a shrimp an' it choked yu praaperly. Yu was always a squeamy little feller. I can't never think 'ow yu managed in the war-time, makin' they shells.

[**LEMMY**, who has brought to the table two mugs and blown the duet out of; them, fills them with port, and hands one to his mother, who is eating her bread and milk.

LEMMY

Ah! Nothin' worried me, 'cept the want o' soap.

MRS LEMMY [Cackling gently]

So it du still, then! Luke at yore face. Yu never was a clean boy, like Jim.

[She puts out a thin finger and touches his cheek, whereon is a black smudge.

LEMMY [Scrubbing his cheek with his sleeve.]
All right! Y'see, I come stryte 'ere, to get rid o' this.

[He drinks.

MRS LEMMY [Eating her bread and milk]
Tes a pity yu'm not got a wife to see't yu wash yureself.

LEMMY [Goggling]
Wife! Not me—I daon't want ter myke no food for pahder. Wot oh!—they said, time o' the war—ye're fightin' for yer children's 'eritage. Well; wot's the 'eritage like, now we've got it? Empty as a shell before yer put the 'igh explosive in. Wot's it like? [Warming to his theme] Like a prophecy in the pypers—not a bit more substantial.

MRS LEMMY [Slightly hypnotised]
How 'e du talk! The gas goes to yore 'ead, I think!

LEMMY
I did the gas to-dy in the cellars of an 'ouse where the wine was mountains 'igh. A regiment couldn't 'a drunk it. Marble pillars in the 'all, butler broad as an observvtion balloon, an' four conscientious khaki footmen. When the guns was roarin' the talk was all for no more o' them glorious weeds-style an' luxury was orf. See wot it is naow. You've got a bare crust in the cupboard 'ere, I works from 'and to mouth in a glutted market—an' there they stand abaht agyne in their britches in the 'oases o' the gryte. I was reg'lar overcome by it. I left a thing in that cellar—I left a thing.... It'll be a bit ork'ard for me to-mower.

[Drinks from his mug.

MRS LEMMY [Placidly, feeling the warmth of the little she has drunk]
What thing?

LEMMY
Wot thing? Old lydy, ye're like a winkle afore yer opens 'er—I never see anything so peaceful. 'Ow dyer manage it?

MRS LEMMY
Settin' 'ere and thenkin'.

LEMMY
Wot abaht?

MRS LEMMY
We-el—Money, an' the works o' God.

LEMMY
Ah! So yer give me a thought sometimes.

MRS LEMMY [Lofting her mug]

Yu ought never to ha' spent yore money on this, Bob!

LEMMY

I thought that meself.

MRS LEMMY

Last time I 'ad a glass o' port wine was the day yore brother Jim went to Ameriky. [Smacking her lips] For a teetotal drink, it du warm 'ee!

LEMMY [Raising his mug]

Well, 'ere's to the British revolution! 'Ere's to the conflygrytion in the sky!

MRS LEMMY [Comfortably]

So as to kape up therr, 'twon't du no 'arm.

[**LEMMY** goes to the window and unhooks his fiddle; he stands with it halfway to his shoulder. Suddenly he opens the window and leans out. A confused murmur of voices is heard; and a snatch of the Marseillaise, sung by a girl. Then the shuffling tramp of feet, and figures are passing in the street.

LEMMY [Turning—excited]

Wot'd I tell yer, old lydy? There it is—there it is!

MRS LEMMY [Placidly]

What is?

LEMMY

The revolution. [He cranes out] They've got it on a barrer. Cheerio!

VOICE [Answering] Cheerio!

LEMMY [Leaning out]

I sy—you 'yn't tykin' the body, are yer?

VOICE

Nao.

LEMMY

Did she die o' starvytion O.K.?

VOICE

She bloomin' well did; I know 'er brother.

LEMMY

Ah! That'll do us a bit o' good!

VOICE

Cheerio!

LEMMY
So long!

VOICE
So long!

[The girl's voice is heard again in the distance singing the Marseillaise. The door is flung open and **LITTLE AIDA** comes running in again.

LEMMY
'Allo, little Aida!

LITTLE AIDA
'Allo, I been follerin' the corfin. It's better than an 'orse dahn!

MRS LEMMY
What coffin?

LITTLE AIDA
Why, 'er's wot died o' starvytion up the street. They're goin' to tyke it to 'Yde Pawk, and 'oller.

MRS LEMMY
Well, never yu mind wot they'm goin' to du: Yu wait an' take my trousers like a gude gell.

[She puts her mug aside and takes up her unfinished pair of trousers. But the wine has entered her fingers, and strength to push the needle through is lacking.

LEMMY [Tuning his fiddle]
Wot'll yer 'ave, little Aida? "Dead March in Saul" or "When the fields was white wiv dysies"?

LITTLE AIDA [With a hop and a brilliant smile]
Aoh yus! "When the fields"—

MRS LEMMY [With a gesture of despair]
Deary me! I 'aven't a-got the strength!

LEMMY
Leave 'em alone, old dear! No one'll be goin' aht wivaht trahsers to-night 'cos yer leaves that one undone. Little Aida, fold 'em up!

[**LITTLE AIDA** methodically folds the five finished pairs of trousers into a pile. **LEMMY** begins playing. A smile comes on the face of **MRS LEMMY**, who is rubbing her fingers. **LITTLE AIDA**, trousers over arm, goes and stares at **LEMMY** playing.

LEMMY [Stopping]
Little Aida, one o' vese dyes yer'll myke an actress. I can see it in yer fyce!

[**LITTLE AIDA** looks at him wide-eyed.

MRS LEMMY
Don't 'ee putt things into 'er 'ead, Bob!

LEMMY
'Tyn't 'er 'ead, old lydy—it's lower. She wants feedin'—feed 'er an' she'll rise. [He strikes into the "Machichi"] Look at 'er naow. I tell yer there's a fortune in 'er.

[**LITTLE AIDA** has put out her tongue.

MRS LEMMY
I'd saner there was a gude 'eart in 'er than any fortune.

LITTLE AIDA [Hugging her pile of trousers]
It's thirteen pence three farthin's I've got to bring yer, an' a penny aht for me, mykes twelve three farthin's: [With the same little hop and sudden smile] I'm goin' to ride back on a bus, I am.

LEMMY
Well, you myke the most of it up there; it's the nearest you'll ever git to 'eaven.

MRS LEMMY
Don' yu discourage 'er, Bob; she'm a gude little thing, an't yu, dear?

LITTLE AIDA [Simply]
Yus.

LEMMY
Not 'arf. Wot c'her do wiv yesterdy's penny?

LITTLE AIDA
Movies.

LEMMY
An' the dy before?

LITTLE AIDA
Movies.

LEMMY
Wot'd I tell yer, old lydy—she's got vicious tystes, she'll finish in the theayter yep Tyke my tip, little Aida; you put every penny into yer foundytions, yer'll get on the boards quicker that wy.

MRS LEMMY
Don' yu pay no 'eed to his talk.

LITTLE AIDA

I daon't.

LEMMY
Would yer like a sip aht o' my mug?

LITTLE AIDA [Brilliant]
Yus.

MRS LEMMY
Not at yore age, me dear, though it is teetotal.

[**LITTLE AIDA** puts her head on one side, like a dog trying to understand.

LEMMY
Well, 'ave one o' my gum-drops.

[Holds out a paper.

[**LITTLE AIDA** brilliant, takes a flat, dark substance from it, and puts it in her mouth.

Give me a kiss, an' I'll give yer a penny.

[**LITTLE AIDA** shakes her head, and leans out of window.

Movver, she daon't know the valyer of money.

MRS LEMMY
Never mind 'im, me dear.

LITTLE AIDA [Sucking the gum-drop—with difficulty]
There's a taxi-cab at the corner.

[**LITTLE AIDA** runs to the door. A figure stands in the doorway; she skids round him and out. **THE PRESS** comes in.

LEMMY [Dubiously]
Wat-oh!

PRESS
Mr. Lemmy?

LEMMY
The syme.

PRESS
I'm from the Press.

LEMMY

Blimy.

PRESS
They told me at your place you wens very likely here.

LEMMY
Yus I left Downin' Street a bit early to-dy!

[He twangs the feddle-strings pompously.

PRESS [Taking out his note-book and writing]
"Fiddles while Rome is burning!" Mr. Lemmy, it's my business at this very critical time to find out what the nation's thinking. Now, as a representative working man—

LEMMY
That's me.

PRESS
You can help me. What are your views?

LEMMY [Putting down fiddle]
Voos? Sit dahn!

[THE PRESS sits on the stool which **LEMMY** has vacated.

The Press—my Muvver. Seventy-seven. She's a wonder; 'yn't yer, old dear?

PRESS
Very happy to make your acquaintance, Ma'am. [He writes] "Mrs. Lemmy, one of the veterans of industry—" By the way, I've jest passed a lot of people following a coffin.

LEMMY
Centre o' the cyclone—cyse o' starvytion; you 'ad 'er in the pyper this mornin'.

PRESS
Ah! yes! Tragic occurrence. [Looking at the trousers.] Hub of the Sweated Industries just here. I especially want to get at the heart—

MRS LEMMY
'Twasn't the 'eart, 'twas the stomach.

PRESS [Writing]
"Mrs. Lemmy goes straight to the point."

LEMMY
Mister, is it my voos or Muvver's yer want?

PRESS

Both.

LEMMY
'Cos if yer get Muvver's, yer won't 'ave time for mine. I tell yer stryte [Confidentially] she's get a glawss a' port wine in 'er. Naow, mind yer, I'm not anxious to be intervooed. On the other 'and, anyfink I might 'eve to sy of valyer—There is a clawss o' politician that 'as nuffn to sy—Aoh! an' daon't 'e sy it just! I dunno wot pyper yer represent.

PRESS [Smiling]
Well, Mr. Lemmy, it has the biggest influ—

LEMMY
They all 'as that; dylies, weeklies, evenin's, Sundyes; but it's of no consequence—my voos are open and aboveboard. Naow, wot shall we begin abaht?

PRESS
Yourself, if you please. And I'd like you to know at once that my paper wants the human note, the real heart-beat of things.

LEMMY
I see; sensytion! Well; 'ere am I—a fustclawss plumber's. assistant—in a job to-dy an' out tomorrer. There's a 'eart-beat in that, I tell yer. 'Oo knows wot the mower 'as for me!

PRESS [Writing]
"The great human issue—Mr. Lemmy touches it at once."

LEMMY
I sy keep my nyme aht o' this; I don' go in fer self-advertisement.

PRESS [Writing]
"True working-man—modest as usual."

LEMMY
I daon't want to embarrass the Gover'ment. They're so ticklish ever since they got the 'abit, war-time, o' mindin' wot people said.

PRESS
Right-o!

LEMMY
For instance, suppose there's goin' to be a revolution—[THE PRESS writes with energy.] 'Ow does it touch me? Like this: I my go up—I cawn't come dahn; no more can Muvver.

MRS LEMMY [Surprisingly]
Us all goes down into the grave.

PRESS
"Mrs. Lemmy interjects the deeper note."

LEMMY

Naow, the gryte—they can come dahn, but they cawn't go up! See! Put two an' two together, an' that's 'ow it touches me. [He utters a throaty laugh] 'Ave yer got that?

PRESS [Quizzical]

Not go up? What about bombs, Mr. Lemmy?

LEMMY [Dubious]

Wot abaht 'em? I s'pose ye're on the comic pypers? 'Ave yer noticed wot a weakness they 'ave for the 'orrible?

PRESS [Writing]

"A grim humour peeped out here and there through the earnestness of his talk."

[He sketches **LEMMY'S** profile.

LEMMY

We 'ad an explosion in my factory time o' the war, that would just ha' done for you comics. [He meditates] Lord! They was after it too,—they an' the Sundyes; but the Censor did 'em. Strike me, I could tell yer things!

PRESS

That's what I want, Mr. Lemmy; tell me things!

LEMMY [Musing]

It's a funny world, 'yn't it? 'Ow we did blow each other up! [Getting up to admire] I sy, I shall be syfe there. That won't betry me anonymiety. Why! I looks like the Prime Minister!

PRESS [Rather hurt]

You were going to tell me things.

LEMMY

Yus, an' they'll be the troof, too.

PRESS

I hope so; we don't—

LEMMY

Wot oh!

PRESS [A little confused.]

We always try to verify—

LEMMY

Yer leave it at tryin', daon't yer? Never, mind, ye're a gryte institootion. Blimy, yer do have jokes, wiv it, spinnin' rahnd on yer own tyles, denyin' to-dy wot ye're goin' to print to-morrer. Ah, well! Ye're like all of us below the line o' comfort—live dyngerously—ever' dy yer last. That's wy I'm interested in the future.

PRESS
Well now—the future. [Writing] "He prophesies."

LEMMY
It's syfer, 'yn't it? [He winks] No one never looks back on prophecies. I remembers an editor spring o' 1916 stykin' his repulytlon the war'd be over in the follerin' October. Increased 'is circulytion abaht 'arf a million by it. 1917 an' war still on—'ad 'is readers gone back on 'im? Nao! They was increasin' like rabbits. Prophesy wot people want to believe, an' ye're syfe. Naow, I'll styke my reputation on somethin', you tyke it dahn word for word. This country's goin' to the dawgs—Naow, 'ere's the sensytion—unless we gets a new religion.

PRESS
Ah! Now for it—yes?

LEMMY
In one word: "Kindness." Daon't mistyke me, nao sickly sentiment and nao patronizin'. Me as kind to the millionaire as 'im to me.

[Fills his mug and drinks.

PRESS [Struck]
That's queer! Kindness! [Writing] "Extremes meet. Bombed and bomber breathing the same music."

LEMMY
But 'ere's the interestin' pynt. Can it be done wivaht blood?

PRESS [Writing]
"He doubts."

LEMMY
No dabt wotever. It cawn't! Blood-and-kindness! Spill the blood o' them that aren't kind—an' there ye are!

PRESS
But pardon me, how are you to tell?

LEMMY
Blimy, they leaps to the heye!

PRESS [Laying down his note-book]
I say, let me talk to you as man to man for a moment.

LEMMY
Orl right. Give it a rest!

PRESS

Your sentiments are familiar to me. I've got a friend on the Press who's very keen on Christ and kindness; and wants to strangle the last king with the—hamstrings of the last priest.

LEMMY [Greatly intrigued]

Not 'arf! Does 'e?

PRESS

Yes. But have you thought it out? Because he hasn't.

LEMMY

The difficulty is—where to stop.

PRESS

Where to begin.

LEMMY

Lawd! I could begin almost anywhere. Why, every month abaht, there's a cove turns me aht of a job 'cos I daon't do just wot 'e likes. They'd 'ave to go. I tell yer stryte—the Temple wants cleanin' up.

PRESS

Ye-es. If I wrote what I thought, I should get the sack as quick as you. D'you say that justifies me in shedding the blood of my boss?

LEMMY

The yaller Press 'as got no blood—'as it? You shed their ile an' vinegar—that's wot you've got to do. Stryte—do yer believe in the noble mission o' the Press?

PRESS

[Enigmatically] Mr. Lemmy, I'm a Pressman.

LEMMY [Goggling]

I see. Not much!

[Gently jogging his mother's elbow.

Wyke up, old lydy!

[For **MRS LEMMY** who has been sipping placidly at her port, is nodding. The evening has drawn in. **LEMMY** strikes a match on his trousers and lights a candle.

Blood an' kindness-that's what's wanted—'specially blood! The 'istory o' me an' my family'll show yer that. Tyke my bruver Fred—crushed by burycrats. Tyke Muvver 'erself. Talk o' the wrongs o' the people! I tell yer the foundytions is rotten. [He empties the bottle into his mother's mug] Daon't mind the mud at the bottom, old lydy—it's all strengthenin'! You tell the Press, Muvver. She can talk abaht the pawst.

PRESS

[Taking up his note-book, and becoming, again his professional self] Yes, Mrs. Lemmy? "Age and Youth—Past and Present—"

MRS LEMMY
Were yu talkin' about Fred? [The port has warmed her veins, the colour in her eyes and cheeks has deepened] My son Fred was always a gude boy—never did nothin' before 'e married. I can see Fred [She bends forward a little in her chair, looking straight before her] acomin' in wi' a pheasant 'e'd found—terrible 'e was at findin' pheasants. When father died, an' yu was cumin', Bob, Fred 'e said to me: "Don't yu never cry, Mother, I'll look after 'ee." An' so 'e did, till 'e married that day six months an' take to the drink in sower. 'E wasn't never 'the same boy again—not Fred. An' now 'e's in That. I can see poor Fred—

[She slowly wipes a tear out of the corner of an eye with the back of her finger.

PRESS [Puzzled]
In—That?

LEMMY [Sotto voce]
Come orf it! Prison! 'S wot she calls it.

MRS LEMMY [Cheerful]
They say life's a vale o' sorrows. Well, so 'tes, but don' du to let yureself thenk so.

PRESS
And so you came to London, Mrs. Lemmy?

MRS LEMMY
Same year as father died. With the four o' them—that's my son Fred, an' my son Jim, an' my son Tom, an' Alice. Bob there, 'e was born in London—an' a praaper time I 'ad of et.

PRESS [Writing]
"Her heroic struggles with poverty—"

MRS LEMMY
Worked in a laundry, I ded, at fifteen shellin's a week, an' brought 'em all up on et till Alice 'ad the gallopin' consumption. I can see poor Alice wi' the little red spots is 'er cheeks—an' I not knowin' wot to du wi' 'her—but I always kept up their buryin' money. Funerals is very dear; Mr. Lemmy was six pound, ten.

PRESS
"High price of Mr. Lemmy."

MRS LEMMY
I've a-got the money for when my time come; never touch et, no matter 'ow things are. Better a little goin' short here below, an' enter the kingdom of 'eaven independent:

PRESS [Writing]
"Death before dishonour—heroine of the slums. Dickens—Betty Higden."

MRS LEMMY

No, sir. Mary Lemmy. I've seen a-many die, I 'ave; an' not one grievin'. I often says to meself: [With a little laugh] "Me dear, when yu go, yu go 'appy. Don' yu never fret about that," I says. An' so I will; I'll go 'appy.

[She stays quite still a moment, and behind her **LEMMY** draws one finger across his face.

MES LEMMY [Smiling]

"Yore old fengers'll 'ave a rest. Think o' that!" I says. "'Twill be a brave change." I can see myself lyin' there an' duin' nothin'.

[Again a pause, while **MRS LEMMY** sees herself doing nothing.

LEMMY

Tell abaht Jim; old lydy.

MRS LEMMY

My son Jim 'ad a family o' seven in six years. "I don' know 'ow 'tes, Mother," 'e used to say to me; "they just sim to come!" That was Jim—never knu from day to day what was cumin'. "Therr's another of 'em dead," 'e used to say, "'tes funny, tu" "Well," I used to say to 'im; "no wonder, poor little things, livin' in they model dwellin's. Therr's no air for 'em," I used to say. "Well," 'e used to say, "what can I du, Mother? Can't afford to live in Park Lane:" An' 'e take an' went to Ameriky. [Her voice for the first time is truly doleful] An' never came back. Fine feller. So that's my four sons—One's dead, an' one's in— That, an' one's in Ameriky, an' Bob 'ere, poor boy, 'e always was a talker.

[**LEMMY**, who has re-seated himself in the window and taken up his fiddle, twangs the strings.

PRESS

And now a few words about your work, Mrs. Lemmy?

MRS LEMMY

Well, I sews.

PRESS [Writing]

"Sews." Yes?

MRS LEMMY [Holding up her unfinished pair of trousers]

I putt in the button'oles, I stretches the flies, I lines the crutch, I putt on this bindin', [She holds up the calico that binds the top] I sews on the buttons, I press the seams—Tuppence three farthin's the pair.

PRESS

Twopence three farthings a pair! Worse than a penny a line!

MRS LEMMY

In a gude day I gets thru four pairs, but they'm gettin' plaguey 'ard for my old fengers.

PRESS [Writing]

"A monumental figure, on whose labour is built the mighty edifice of our industrialism."

LEMMY
I sy—that's good. Yer'll keep that, won't yet?

MRS LEMMY
I finds me own cotton, tuppence three farthin's, and other expension is a penny three farthin's.

PRESS
And are you an exception, Mrs. Lemmy?

MRS LEMMY
What's that?

LEMMY
Wot price the uvvers, old lydy? Is there a lot of yer sewin' yer fingers orf at tuppence 'ypenny the pair?

MRS LEMMY
I can't tell yu that. I never sees nothin' in 'ere. I pays a penny to that little gell to bring me a dozen pair an' fetch 'em back. Poor little thing, she'm 'ardly strong enough to carry 'em. Feel! They'm very 'eavy!

PRESS
On the conscience of Society!

LEMMY
I sy put that dahn, won't yer?

PRESS
Have things changed much since the war, Mrs. Lemmy?

MRS LEMMY
Cotton's a lot dearer.

PRESS
All round, I mean.

MRS LEMMY
Aw! Yu don' never get no change, not in my profession. [She oscillates the trousers] I've a-been in trousers fifteen year; ever since I got to old for laundry.

PRESS [Writing]
"For fifteen years sewn trousers." What would a good week be, Mrs. Lemmy?

MRS LEMMY
'Tes a very gude week, five shellin's.

LEMMY [From the window]
Bloomin' millionairess, Muvver. She's lookin' forward to 'eaven, where vey don't wear no trahsers.

MRS LEMMY [With spirit]

'Tidn for me to zay whether they du. An' 'tes on'y when I'm a bit low-sperrity-like as I wants to go therr. What I am a-lukin' forward to, though, 'tes a day in the country. I've not a-had one since before the war. A kind lady brought me in that bit of 'eather; 'tes wonderful sweet stuff when the 'oney's in et. When I was a little gell I used to zet in the 'eather gatherin' the whorts, an' me little mouth all black wi' eatin' them. 'Twas in the 'eather I used to zet, Sundays, courtin'. All flesh is grass—an' 'tesn't no bad thing—grass.

PRESS [Writing]

"The old paganism of the country." What is your view of life, Mrs. Lemmy?

LEMMY [Suddenly]

Wot is 'er voo of life? Shall I tell yer mine? Life's a disease—a blinkin' oak-apple! Daon't myke no mistyke. An' 'umen life's a yumourous disease; that's all the difference. Why—wot else can it be? See the bloomin' promise an' the blighted performance—different as a 'eadline to the noos inside. But yer couldn't myke Muvver see vat—not if yer talked to 'er for a wok. Muvver still believes in fings. She's a country gell; at a 'undred and fifty she'll be a country gell, won't yer, old lydy?

MRS LEMMY

Well, 'tesn't never been 'ome to me in London. I lived in the country forty year—I did my lovin' there; I buried father therr. Therr bain't nothin' in life, yu know, but a bit o' lovin'—all said an' done; bit o' lovin', with the wind, an' the stars out.

LEMMY [In a loud apologetic whisper]

She 'yn't often like this. I told yer she'd got a glawss o' port in 'er.

MRS LEMMY

'Tes a brave pleasure, is lovin'. I likes to zee et in young folk. I likes to zee 'em kissin'; shows the 'eart in 'em. 'Tes the 'eart makes the world go round; 'tesn't nothin' else, in my opinion.

PRESS [Writing]

"—sings the swan song of the heart."—

MRS LEMMY [Overhearing]

No, I never yeard a swan sing—never! But I tell 'ee what I 'eve 'eard; the Bells singin' in th' orchard 'angin' up the clothes to dry, an' the cuckoos callin' back to 'em. [Smiling] There's a-many songs in the country-the 'eart is freelike in th' country!

LEMMY [Soto voce]

Gi' me the Strand at ar' past nine.

PRESS [Writing]

"Town and country—"

MRS LEMMY

'Tidn't like that in London; one day's jest like another. Not but what therr's a 'eap o' kind'eartedness 'ere.

LEMMY [Gloomily]

Kind-'eartedness! I daon't fink "Boys an' Gells come out to play."

[He plays the old tune on his fiddle.

MRS LEMMY [Singing]

"Boys an' Gells come out to play. The mune is shinin' bright as day." [She laughs] I used to sing like a lark when I was a gell.

[**LITTLE AIDA** enters.

LITTLE AIDA

There's 'undreds follerin' the corfin. 'Yn't you goin', Mr. Lemmy—it's dahn your wy!

LEMMY [Dubiously]

Well yus—I s'pose they'll miss me.

LITTLE AIDA

Aoh! Tyke me!

PRESS

What's this?

LEMMY

The revolution in 'Yde Pawk.

PRESS [Struck]

In Hyde Park? The very thing. I'll take you down. My taxi's waiting.

LITTLE AIDA

Yus; it's breathin' 'ard, at the corner.

PRESS [Looking at his watch]

Ah! and Mrs. Lemmy. There's an Anti-Sweating Meeting going on at a house in Park Lane. We can get there in twenty minutes if we shove along. I want you to tell them about the trouser-making. You'll be a sensation!

LEMMY [To himself]

Sensytion! 'E cawn't keep orf it!

MRS LEMMY

Anti-Sweat. Poor fellers! I 'ad one come to see we before the war, an' they'm still goin' on? Wonderful, an't it?

PRESS

Come, Mrs. Lemmy; drive in a taxi, beautiful moonlit night; and they'll give you a splendid cup of tea.

MRS LEMMY [Unmoved]

Ah! I cudn't never du without my tea. There's not an avenin' but I thinks to meself: Now, me dear, yu've a-got one more to fennish, an' then yu'll 'eve yore cup o' tea. Thank you for callin', all the same.

LEMMY

Better siccumb to the temptytion, old lydy; joyride wiv the Press; marble floors, pillars o' gold; conscientious footmen; lovely lydies; scuppers runnin' tea! An' the revolution goin' on across the wy. 'Eaven's nuffink to Pawk Lyne.

PRESS

Come along, Mrs. Lemmy!

MRS LEMMY [Seraphically]

Thank yu,—I'm a-feelin' very comfortable. 'Tes wonderful what a drop o' wine'll du for the stomach.

PRESS

A taxi-ride!

MRS LEMMY [Placidly]

Ah! I know'em. They'm very busy things.

LEMMY

Muvver shuns notority. [Sotto voce to **THE PRESS**] But you watch me! I'll rouse 'er.

[He takes up his fiddle and sits on the window seat. Above the little houses on the opposite side of the street, the moon has risen in the dark blue sky, so that the cloud shaped like a beast seems leaping over it. **LEMMY** plays the first notes of the Marseillaise. A black cat on the window-sill outside looks in, hunching its back. **LITTLE AIDA** barks at her. **MRS LEMMY** struggles to her feet, sweeping the empty dish and spoon to the floor in the effort.

The dish ran awy wiv the spoon! That's right, old lydy!

[He stops playing.]

MRS LEMMY [Smiling, and moving her hands]

I like a bit o' music. It du that move 'ee.

PRESS

Bravo, Mrs. Lemmy. Come on!

LEMMY

Come on, old dear! We'll be in time for the revolution yet.

MRS LEMMY

'Tes 'earin' the Old 'Undred again!

LEMMY [To **THE PRESS**]

She 'yn't been aht these two years. [To his **MOTHER**, who has put up her hands to her head] Nao, never mind yer 'at. [To **THE PRESS**] She 'yn't got none! [Aloud] No West-End lydy wears anyfink at all in the evenin'!

MRS LEMMY
'Ow'm I lukin', Bob?

LEMMY
First-clawss; yer've got a colour fit to toast by. We'll show 'em yer've got a kick in yer. [He takes her arm] Little Aida, ketch 'old o' the sensytions.

[He indicates the trousers **THE PRESS** takes **MRS LEMMY'S** other arm.]

MRS LEMMY [With an excited little laugh]
Quite like a gell!

[And, smiling between her son and **THE PRESS**, she passes out; **LITTLE AIDA**, with a fling of her heels and a wave of the trousers, follows.

CURTAIN

ACT III

An octagon ante-room of the hall at Lord William Dromondy's. A shining room lighted by gold candelabra, with gold-curtained pillars, through which the shining hall and a little of the grand stairway are visible. A small table with a gold-coloured cloth occupies the very centre of the room, which has a polished parquet floor and high white walls. Gold-coloured doors on the left. Opposite these doors a window with gold-coloured curtains looks out on Park Lane. **LADY WILLIAM** standing restlessly between the double doors and the arch which leads to the hall. **JAMES** is stationary by the double doors, from behind which come sounds of speech and applause.

POULDER [Entering from the hall]
His Grace the Duke of Exeter, my lady.

[**HIS GRACE** enters. He is old, and youthful, with a high colour and a short rough white beard. **LADY WILLIAM** advances to meet him. **POULDER** stands by.

LADY WILLIAM
Oh! Father, you ARE late.

HIS GRACE
Awful crowd in the streets, Nell. They've got a coffin—couldn't get by.

LADY WILLIAM
Coin? Whose?

HIS GRACE

The Government's I should think—no flowers, by request. I say, have I got to speak?

LADY WILLIAM

Oh! no, dear.

HIS GRACE

H'm! That's unlucky. I've got it here. [He looks down his cuff] Found something I said in 1914—just have done.

LADY WILLIAM

Oh! If you've got it—James, ask Lord William to come to me for a moment. [**JAMES** vanishes through the door. To **THE DUKE**] Go in, Grand-dad; they'll be so awfully pleased to see you. I'll tell Bill.

HIS GRACE

Where's Anne?

LADY WILLIAM

In bed, of course.

HIS GRACE

I got her this—rather nice?

[He has taken from his breast-pocket one of those street toy-men that jump head over heels on your hand; he puts it through its paces.

LADY WILLIAM [Much interested]

Oh! no, but how sweet! She'll simply love it.

POULDER

If I might suggest to Your Grace to take it in and operate it. It's sweated, Your Grace. They-er-make them in those places.

HIS GRACE

By Jove! D'you know the price, Poulder?

POULDER [Interrogatively]

A penny, is it? Something paltry, Your Grace!

HIS GRACE

Where's that woman who knows everything; Miss Munday?

LADY WILLIAM

Oh! She'll be in there, somewhere.

[**HIS GRACE** moves on, and passes through the doors. The sound of applause is heard.

POULDER [Discreetly]

Would you care to see the bomb, my lady?

LADY WILLIAM
Of course—first quiet moment.

POULDER
I'll bring it up, and have a watch put on it here, my lady.

[**LORD WILLIAM** comes through the double doom followed by **JAMES. POULDER** retires.

LORD WILLIAM
Can't you come, Nell?

LADY WILLIAM
Oh! Bill, your Dad wants to speak.

LORD WILLIAM
The deuce he does—that's bad.

LADY WILLIAM
Yes, of course, but you must let him; he's found something he said in 1914.

LORD WILLIAM
I knew it. That's what they'll say. Standing stock still, while hell's on the jump around us.

LADY WILLIAM
Never mind that; it'll please him; and he's got a lovely little sweated toy that turns head over heels at one penny.

LORD WILLIAM
H'm! Well, come on.

LADY WILLIAM
No, I must wait for stragglers. There's sure to be an editor in a hurry.

POULDER [Announcing]
Mis-ter Gold-rum!

LADY WILLIAM [Sotto voce]
And there he is!

[She advances to meet a thin, straggling man in eyeglasses, who is smiling absently.

How good of you!

MR G
Thanks awfully. I just er—and then I'm afraid I must—er—Things look very—Thanks—Thanks so much.

[He straggles through the doors, and is enclosed by **JAMES**.]

POULDER
Miss Mun-day.

LORD WILLIAM
There! I thought she was in—She really is the most unexpected woman! How do you do? How awfully sweet of you!

MISS MUNDAY [An elderly female schoolboy]
How do you do? There's a spiffing crowd. I believe things are really going Bolshy. How do you do, Lord William? Have you got any of our people to show? I told one or two, in case—they do so simply love an outing.

JAMES
There are three old chips in the lobby, my Lord.

LORD WILLIAM
What? Oh! I say! Bring them in at once. Why—they're the hub of the whole thing.

JAMES [Going]
Very good, my Lord.

LADY WILLIAM
I am sorry. I'd no notion; and they're such dears always.

MISS MUNDAY
I must tell you what one of them said to me. I'd told him not to use such bad language to his wife. "Don't you worry, Ma!" he said, "I expert you can do a bit of that yourself!"

LADY WILLIAM
How awfully nice! It's SO like them.

MISS MUNDAY
Yes. They're wonderful.

LORD WILLIAM
I say, why do we always call them they?

LADY WILLIAM
[Puzzled] Well, why not?

LORD WILLIAM
THEY!

MISS MUNDAY [Struck]
Quite right, Lord William! Quite right! Another species. They! I must remember that. THEY!

[She passes on.

LADY WILLIAM [About to follow]
Well, I don't see; aren't they?

LORD WILLIAM
Never mind, old girl; follow on. They'll come in with me.

[**MISS MUNDAY** and **LADY WILLIAM** pass through the double doors.

POULDER [Announcing]
Some sweated workers, my Lord.

[There enter a tall, thin, oldish woman; a short, thin, very lame man, her husband; and a stoutish middle-aged woman with a rolling eye and gait, all very poorly dressed, with lined and heated faces.]

LORD WILLIAM [Shaking hands]
How d'you do! Delighted to see you all. It's awfully good of you to have come.

LAME MAN
Mr. and Mrs. Tomson. We 'ad some trouble to find it. You see, I've never been in these parts. We 'ad to come in the oven; and the bus-bloke put us dahn wrong. Are you the proprietor?

LORD WILLIAM [Modestly]
Yes, I—er—

LAME MAN
You've got a nice plyce. I says to the missis, I says: "'E's got a nice plyce 'ere," I says; "there's room to turn rahnd."

LORD WILLIAM
Yes—shall we—?

LAME MAN
An' Mrs. Annaway she says: "Shouldn't mind livin 'ere meself," she says; "but it must cost'im a tidy penny," she says.

LORD WILLIAM
It does—it does; much too tidy. Shall we—?

MRS ANN [Rolling her eye]
I'm very pleased to 'ave come. I've often said to 'em: "Any time you want me," I've said, "I'd be pleased to come."

LORD WILLIAM
Not so pleased as we are to see you.

MRS ANN

I'm sure you're very kind.

JAMES [From the double doors, through which he has received a message]
Wanted for your speech, my Lord.

LORD WILLIAM
Oh! God! Poulder, bring these ladies and gentleman in, and put them where everybody can—where they can see everybody, don't you know.

[He goes out hurriedly through the double doors.

LAME MAN
Is 'e a lord?

POULDER
He is. Follow me.

[He moves towards the doors, the three workers follow.]

MRS ANN [Stopping before **JAMES**]
You 'yn't one, I suppose?

[**JAMES** stirs no muscle.

POULDER
Now please. [He opens the doors. The Voice of **LORD WILLIAM** speaking is heard] Pass in.

[**THE THREE WORKERS** pass in, **POULDER** and **JAMES** follow them. The doors are not closed, and through this aperture comes the voice of **LORD WILLIAM**, punctuated and supported by decorous applause.

[**LITTLE ANNE** runs in, and listens at the window to the confused and distant murmurs of a **CROWD**.

VOICE OF LORD WILLIAM
We propose to move for a further advance in the chain-making and—er—er—match-box industries.

[Applause.

[**LITTLE ANNE** runs across to the door, to listen.]

VOICE OF LORD WILLIAM [On rising voice] I would conclude with some general remarks. Ladies and gentlemen, the great natural, but—er—artificial expansion which trade experienced the first years after the war has—er—collapsed. These are hard times. We who are fortunate feel more than ever—er—responsible—[He stammers, loses the thread of his thoughts.]—[Applause]—er—responsible—[The thread still eludes him]—er—

LITTLE ANNE [Poignantly]
Oh, Daddy!

LORD WILLIAM [Desperately]
In fact—er—you know how—er—responsible we feel.

LITTLE ANNE
Hooray!

[Applause.

[There float in through the windows the hoarse and distant sounds of the Marseillaise, as sung by London voices.

LORD WILLIAM
There is a feeling in the air—that I for one should say deliberately was—er—a feeling in the air—er—a feeling in the air—

LITTLE ANNE [Agonised]
Oh, Daddy! Stop!

[JAMES enters, and closes the door behind him.

JAMES
Look here! 'Ave I got to report you to Miss Stokes?]

LITTLE ANNE
No-o-o!

JAMES
Well, I'm goin' to.

LITTLE ANNE
Oh, James, be a friend to me! I've seen nothing yet.

JAMES
No; but you've eaten a good bit, on the stairs. What price that Peach Melba?

LITTLE ANNE
I can't go to bed till I've digested it can I? There's such a lovely crowd in the street!

JAMES
Lovely? Ho!

LITTLE ANNE [Wheedling]
James, you couldn't tell Miss Stokes! It isn't in you, is it?

JAMES [Grinning]
That's right.

LITTLE ANNE
So-I'll just get under here.

[She gets under the table.

Do I show?

JAMES [Stooping]
Not 'arf!

[**POULDER** enters from the hall.

POULDER
What are you doin' there?

JAMES [Between him and the table—raising himself]
Thinkin'.

[**POULDER** purses his mouth to repress his feedings.

POULDER
My orders are to fetch the bomb up here for Lady William to inspect. Take care no more writers stray in.

JAMES
How shall I know 'em?

POULDER
Well—either very bald or very hairy.

JAMES
Right-o!

[He goes.

[**POULDER**, with his back to the table, busies himself with the set of his collar.

POULDER [Addressing an imaginary audience—in a low but important voice]
The—ah—situation is seerious. It is up to us of the—ah—leisured classes—

[The face of **LITTLE ANNE** is poked out close to his legs, and tilts upwards in wonder towards the bow of his waistcoat.

—to—ah—keep the people down. The olla polloi are clamourin'—

[**MISS STOKES** appears from the hall, between the pillars.

Miss S. Poulder!

POULDER [Making a volte face towards the table]
Miss?

MISS STOKES
Where is Anne?

POULDER [Vexed at the disturbance of his speech]
Excuse me, Miss—to keep track of Miss Anne is fortunately no part of my dooties.

MISS STOKES
She really is naughty.

POULDER
She is. If she was mine, I'd spank her.

[The smiling face of **LITTLE ANNE** becomes visible again close to his legs.

MISS STOKES
Not a nice word.

POULDER
No; but a pleasant haction. Miss Anne's the limit. In fact, Lord and Lady William are much too kind
'earted all round. Take these sweated workers; that class o' people are quite 'opeless. Treatin' them as
your equals, shakin 'ands with 'em, givin 'em tea—it only puffs 'em out. Leave it to the Church, I say.

MISS STOKES
The Church is too busy, Poulder.

POULDER
Ah! That "Purity an' Future o' the Race Campaign." I'll tell you what I thinks the danger o' that, Miss. So
much purity that there won't be a future race. [Expanding] Purity of 'eart's an excellent thing, no doubt,
but there's a want of nature about it. Same with this Anti-Sweating. Unless you're anxious to come
down, you must not put the lower classes up.

MISS STOKES
I don't agree with you at all, Poulder.

POULDER
Ah! You want it both ways, Miss. I should imagine you're a Liberal.

MISS STOKES [Horrified]
Oh, no! I certainly am not.

POULDER
Well, I judged from your takin' cocoa. Funny thing that, about cocoa-how it still runs through the Liberal
Party! It's virtuous, I suppose. Wine, beer, tea, coffee-all of 'em vices. But cocoa you might drink a
gallon a day and annoy no one but yourself! There's a lot o' deep things in life, Miss!

MISS STOKES
Quite so. But I must find Anne.

[She recedes.

POULDER [Suavely]
Well, I wish you every success; and I hope you'll spank her. This modern education—there's no fruitiness in it.

LITTLE ANNE [From under the table]
Poulder, are you virtuous?

POULDER [Jumping]
Good Ged!

LITTLE ANNE
D'you mind my asking? I promised James I would.

POULDER
Miss Anne, come out!

[The four **FOOTMEN** appear in the hall, **HENRY** carrying the wine cooler.

JAMES
Form fours-by your right-quick march!

[They enter, marching down right of table.

Right incline—Mark time! Left turn! 'Alt! 'Enry, set the bomb! Stand easy!

[**HENRY** places the wine cooler on the table and covers it with a blue embroidered Chinese mat, which has occupied the centre of the tablecloth.

POULDER
Ah! You will 'ave your game! Thomas, take the door there! James, the 'all! Admit titles an' bishops. No literary or Labour people. Charles and 'Enry, 'op it and 'ang about!

[**CHARLES** and **HENRY** go out, the other too move to their stations.

[**POULDER**, stands by the table looking at the covered bomb. The hoarse and distant sounds of the Marseillaise float in again from Park Lane.

POULDER [Moved by some deep feeling]
And this house an 'orspital in the war! I ask you—what was the good of all our sacrifices for the country? No town 'ouse for four seasons—rustygettin' in the shires, not a soul but two boys under me. Lord William at the front, Lady William at the back. And all for this! [He points sadly at the cooler] It comes of meddlin' on the Continent. I had my prognostications at the time. [To **JAMES**] You remember my

sayin' to you just before you joined up: "Mark my words—we shall see eight per cent. for our money before this is over!"

JAMES [Sepulchrally]
I see the eight per cent., but not the money.

POULDER
Hark at that!

[The sounds of the Marseillaise grow louder. He shakes his head.

I'd read the Riot Act. They'll be lootin' this house next!

JAMES
We'll put up a fight over your body: "Bartholomew Poulder, faithful unto death!" Have you insured your life?

POULDER
Against a revolution?

JAMES
Act o' God! Why not?

POULDER
It's not an act o' God.

JAMES
It is; and I sympathise with it.

POULDER
You—what?

JAMES
I do—only—hands off the gov'nor.

POULDER
Oh! Really! Well, that's something. I'm glad to see you stand behind him, at all events.

JAMES
I stand in front of 'im when the scrap begins!

POULDER
Do you insinuate that my heart's not in the right place?

JAMES
Well, look at it! It's been creepin' down ever since I knew you. Talk of your sacrifices in the war—they put you on your honour, and you got stout on it. Rations—not 'arf.

POULDER [Staring at him]

For independence, I've never seen your equal, James. You might be an Australian.

JAMES [Suavely]

Keep a civil tongue, or I'll throw you to the crowd! [He comes forward to the table] Shall I tell you why I favour the gov'nor? Because, with all his pomp, he's a gentleman, as much as I am. Never asks you to do what he wouldn't do himself. What's more, he never comes it over you. If you get drunk, or—well, you understand me, Poulder—he'll just say: "Yes, yes; I know, James!" till he makes you feel he's done it himself. [Sinking his voice mysteriously] I've had experience with him, in the war and out. Why he didn't even hate the Huns, not as he ought. I tell you he's no Christian.

POULDER

Well, for irreverence—!

JAMES [Obstinately]

And he'll never be. He's got too soft a heart.

LITTLE ANNE [Beneath the table-shrilly]

Hurrah!

POULDER [Jumping]

Come out, Miss Anne!

JAMES

Let 'er alone!

POULDER

In there, under the bomb?

JAMES [Contemptuously]

Silly ass! You should take 'em lying down!

POULDER

Look here, James! I can't go on in this revolutionary spirit; either you or I resign.

JAMES

Crisis in the Cabinet!

POULDER

I give you your marchin' orders.

JAMES [Ineffably]

What's that you give me?

POULDER

Thomas, remove James!

[**THOMAS** grins.

LITTLE ANNE [Who, with open mouth, has crept out to see the fun]
Oh! Do remove James, Thomas!

POULDER
Go on, Thomas.

[**THOMAS** takes one step towards **JAMES**, who lays a hand on the Chinese mat covering the bomb.]

JAMES [Grimly]
If I lose control of meself.

LITTLE ANNE [Clapping her hands]
Oh! James! Do lose control! Then I shall see it go off!

JAMES [To **POULDER**]
Well, I'll merely empty the pail over you!

POULDER
This is not becomin'!

[He walks out into the hall.

JAMES
Another strategic victory! What a Boche he'd have made. As you were, Tommy!

[**THOMAS** returns to the door. The sound of prolonged applause cornea from within.

That's a bishop.

LITTLE ANNE
Why?

JAMES
By the way he's drawin'. It's the fine fightin' spirit in 'em. They were the backbone o' the war. I see there's a bit o' the old stuff left in you, Tommy.

LITTLE ANNE [Scrutinizing the widely—grinning **THOMAS**]
Where? Is it in his mouth?

JAMES
You've still got a sense of your superiors. Didn't you notice how you moved to Poulder's orders, me boy; an' when he was gone, to mine?

LITTLE ANNE [To **THOMAS**]
March!

[The grinning **THOMAS** remains immovable.

He doesn't, James!

JAMES
Look here, Miss Anne—your lights ought to be out before ten. Close in, Tommy!

[He and **THOMAS** move towards her.]

LITTLE ANNE [Dodging]
Oh, no! Oh, no! Look!

[The **FOOTMEN** stop and turn. There between the pillars, stands **LITTLE AIDA** with the trousers, her face brilliant With surprise.

JAMES
Good Lord! What's this?

[Seeing **LITTLE ANNE, LITTLE AIDA** approaches, fascinated, and the two children sniff at each other as it were like two little dogs walking round and round.

LITTLE ANNE [Suddenly]
My name's Anne; what's yours?

LITTLE AIDA
Aida.

LITTLE ANNE
Are you lost?

LITTLE AIDA
Nao.

LITTLE ANNE
Are those trousers?

LITTLE AIDA
Yus.

LITTLE ANNIE
 Whose?

LITTLE AIDA
Mrs Lemmy's.

LITTLE ANNE
Does she wear them?

[**LITTLE AIDA** smiles brilliantly.

LITTLE AIDA
Nao. She sews 'em.

LITTLE ANNE [Touching the trousers]
They are hard. James's are much softer; aren't they, James? [**JAMES** deigns no reply] What shall we do? Would you like to see my bedroom?

LITTLE AIDA [With a hop]
Aoh, yus!

JAMES
No.

LITTLE ANNE
Why not?

JAMES
Have some sense of what's fittin'.

LITTLE ANNE
Why isn't it fittin'? [To **LITTLE AIDA**] Do you like me?

LITTLE AIDA
Yus-s.

LITTLE ANNE
So do I. Come on!

[She takes **LITTLE AIDA'S** hand.

JAMES [Between the pillars]
Tommy, ketch 'em!

[**THOMAS** retains them by the skirts.

LITTLE ANNE [Feigning indifference]
All right, then! [To **LITTLE AIDA**] Have you ever seen a bomb?

LITTLE AIDA
Nao.

LITTLE ANNE [Going to the table and lifting a corner of the cover]
Look!

LITTLE AIDA [Looking]
What's it for?

LITTLE ANNE
To blow up this house.

LITTLE AIDA
I daon't fink!

LITTLE ANNE
Why not?

LITTLE AIDA
It's a beautiful big 'Ouse.

LITTLE ANNE
That's why. Isn't it, James?

LITTLE AIDA
You give the fing to me; I'll blow up our 'ouse—it's an ugly little 'ouse.

LITTLE ANNE [Struck]
Let's all blow up our own; then we can start fair. Daddy would like that.

LITTLE AIDA
Yus. [Suddenly brilliant] I've 'ad a ride in a taxi, an' we're goin' 'ome in it agyne!

LITTLE ANNE
Were you sick?

LITTLE AIDA [Brilliant]
Nao.

LITTLE ANNE
I was; when I first went in one, but I was quite young then. James, could you get her a Peche Melba? There was one.

JAMES
No.

LITTLE ANNE
Have you seen the revolution?

LITTLE AIDA
Wot's that?

LITTLE ANNE
It's made of people.

LITTLE AIDA
I've seen the corfin, it's myde o' wood.

LITTLE ANNE
Do you hate the rich?

LITTLE AIDA [Ineffably]
Nao. I hates the poor.

LITTLE ANNE
Why?

LITTLE AIDA
'Cos they 'yn't got nuffin'.

LITTLE ANNE
I love the poor. They're such dears.

LITTLE AIDA [Shaking her head with a broad smile]
Nao.

LITTLE ANNE
Why not?

LITTLE AIDA
I'd tyke and lose the lot, I would.

LITTLE ANNE
Where?

LITTLE AIDA
In the water.

LITTLE ANNE
Like puppies?

LITTLE AIDA
Yus.

LITTLE ANNE
Why?

LITTLE AIDA
Then I'd be shut of 'em.

LITTLE ANNE [Puzzled]
Oh!

[The voice of **THE PRESS** is heard in the hall. "Where's the little girl?"]

JAMES
That's you. Come 'ere!

[He puts a hand behind **LITTLE AIDA'S** back and propels her towards the hall. **THE PRESS** enters with old **MRS LEMMY**.

PRESS
Oh! Here she is, major domo. I'm going to take this old lady to the meeting; they want her on the platform. Look after our friend, Mr. Lemmy here; Lord William wants to see him presently.

LITTLE ANNE [In an awed whisper]
James, it's the little blighter!

[She dives again under the table. **LEMMY** enters.

LEMMY
'Ere! 'Arf a mo'! Yer said yer'd drop me at my plyce. Well, I tell yer candid—this 'yn't my plyce.

PRESS
That's all right, Mr. Lemmy. [He grins] They'll make you wonderfully comfortable, won't you, major domo?

[He passes on through the room, to the door, ushering old **MRS LEMMY** and **LITTLE AIDA**.

[**POULDER** blocks **LEMMY'S** way, with **CHARLES** and **HENRY** behind him.

POULDER
James, watch it; I'll report.

[He moves away, following **THE PRESS** through the door. **JAMES** between table and window. **THOMAS** has gone to the door. **HENRY** and **CHARLES** remain at the entrances to the hall. **LEMMY** looks dubiously around, his cockney assurrance gradually returns.

LEMMY
I think I knows the gas 'ere. This is where I came to-dy, 'yn't it? Excuse my hesitytion—these little 'ouses IS so much the syme.

JAMES [Gloomily]
They are!

LEMMY [Looking at the four immovable **FOOTMEN**, till he concentrates on **JAMES**]
Ah! I 'ad a word wiv you, 'adn't I? You're the four conscientious ones wot's wyin' on your gov'nor's chest. 'Twas you I spoke to, wasn't it? [His eyes travel over them again] Ye're so monotonous. Well, ye're busy now, I see. I won't wyste yer time.

[He turns towards the hall, but **CHARLES** and **HENRY** bar the way in silence.

[Skidding a little, and regarding the four immovables once more.

LEMMY

I never see such pytient men? Compared wiv yer, mountains is restless.

[He goes to the table. **JAMES** watches him. **ANNE** barks from underneath.

LEMMY [Skidding again]

Why! There's a dawg under there. [Noting the grin on **THOMAS'S** face] Glad it amooses yer. Yer want it, daon't yer, wiv a fyce like that? Is this a ply wivaht words? 'Ave I got into the movies by mistyke? Turn aht, an' let's 'ave six penn'orth o' darkness.

LITTLE ANNE [From beneath the Table]

No, no! Not dark!

LEMMY [Musingly]

The dawg talks anywy. Come aht, Fido!

[**LITTLE ANNE** emerges, and regards him with burning curiosity.

LEMMY

Is this the lytest fashion o' receivin' guests?

LITTLE ANNE

Mother always wants people to feel at home. What shall we do? Would you like to hear the speeches? Thomas, open the door a little, do!

JAMES

'Umour 'er a couple o' inches, Tommy!

[**THOMAS** draws the door back stealthily an inch or so.

LITTLE ANNE [After applying her eye-in a loud whisper]

There's the old lady. Daddy's looking at her trousers. Listen!

[For **MRS LEMMY'S** voice is floating faintly through: "I putt in the buttonholes, I stretches the flies; I 'ems the bottoms; I lines the crutch; I putt on this bindin'; I sews on the buttons; I presses the seams—Tuppence three farthin's the pair."

LEMMY [In a hoarse whisper]

That's it, old lydy: give it 'em!

LITTLE ANNE

Listen!

VOICE OF LORD WILLIAM

We are indebted to our friends the Press for giving us the pleasure—er—pleasure of hearing from her own lips—the pleasure—

LITTLE ANNE
Oh! Daddy!

[**THOMAS** abruptly closes the doors.

LEMMY [To **LITTLE ANNE**]
Now yer've done it. See wot comes o' bein' impytient. We was just gettin' to the marrer.

LITTLE ANNE
What can we do for you now?

LEMMY [Pointing to **LITTLE ANNE**, and addressing **JAMES**]
Wot is this one, anywy?

JAMES [Sepulchrally]
Daughter o' the house.

LEMMY
Is she insured agynst 'er own curiosity?

LITTLE ANNE
Why?

LEMMY
As I daon't believe in a life beyond the gryve, I might be tempted to send yer there.

LITTLE ANNE
What is the gryve?

LEMMY
Where little gells goes to.

LITTLE ANNE
Oh, when?

LEMMY [Pretending to look at a match, which is not there]
Well, I dunno if I've got time to finish yer this minute. Sy to-mower at. 'arf past.

LITTLE ANNE
Half past what?

LEMMY [Despairingly]
'Arf past wot!

[The sound of applause is heard.

JAMES
That's 'is Grace. 'E's gettin' wickets, too.

[**POULDER** entering from the door.

POULDER
Lord William is slippin' in.

[He makes a cabalistic sign with his head. Jeers crosses to the door. **LEMMY** looks dubiously at **POULDER**.

LEMMY [Suddenly—as to himself]
Wot oh! I am the portly one!

POULDER [Severely]
Any such allusion aggeravates your offence.

LEMMY
Oh, ah! Look 'ere, it was a corked bottle. Now, tyke care, tyke care, 'aughty! Daon't curl yer lip! I shall myke a clean breast o' my betryal when the time comes!

[There is a alight movement of the door. **ANNE** makes a dive towards the table but is arrested by **POULDER** grasping her waistband. **LORD WILLIAM** slips in, followed by **THE PRESS**, on whom **JAMES** and **THOMAS** close the door too soon.

HALF OF THE PRESS [Indignantly]
Look out!

JAMES
Do you want him in or out, me Lord?

LEMMY
I sy, you've divided the Press; 'e was unanimous.

[The **FOOTMEN** let **THE PRESS** through.

LORD WILLIAM [To **THE PRESS**]
I'm so sorry.

LEMMY
Would yer like me to see to 'is gas?

LORD WILLIAM
So you're my friend of the cellars?

LEMMY [Uneasy]
I daon't deny it.

[**POULDER** begins removing **LITTLE ANNE**.

LITTLE ANNE

Let me stay, Daddy; I haven't seen anything yet! If I go, I shall only have to come down again when they loot the house. Listen!

[The hoarse strains of the Marseillaise are again heard from the distance.

LORD WILLIAM [Blandly]

Take her up, Poulder!

LITTLE ANNE

Well, I'm coming down again—and next time I shan't have any clothes on, you know.

[They vanish between the pillars. **LORD WILLIAM** makes a sign of dismissal. The **FOOTMAN** file out.

LEMMY [Admiringly]

Luv'ly pyces!

LORD WILLIAM [Pleasantly]

Now then; let's have our talk, Mr.—

LEMMY

Lemmy.

PRESS [Who has slipped his note-book out]

"Bombed and Bomber face to face—"

LEMMY [Uneasy]

I didn't come 'ere agyne on me own, yer know. The Press betryed me.

LORD WILLIAM

Is that old lady your mother?

LEMMY

The syme. I tell yer stryte, it was for 'er I took that old bottle o' port. It was orful old.

LORD WILLIAM

Ah! Port? Probably the '83. Hope you both enjoyed it.

LEMMY

So far-yus. Muvver'll suffer a bit tomower, I expect.

LORD WILLIAM

I should like to do something for your mother, if you'll allow me.

LEMMY

Oh! I'll allow yer. But I dunno wot she'll sy.

LORD WILLIAM

I can see she's a fine independent old lady! But suppose you were to pay her ten bob a week, and keep my name out of it?

LEMMY
Well, that's one wy o' YOU doin' somefink, 'yn't it?

LORD WILLIAM
I giving you the money, of course.

PRESS [Writing]
"Lord William, with kingly generosity—"

LEMMY [Drawing attention to **THE PRESS** with his thumb]
I sy—I daon't mind, meself—if you daon't—

LORD WILLIAM
He won't write anything to annoy me.

PRESS
This is the big thing, Lord William; it'll get the public bang in the throat.

LEMMY [Confidentially]
Bit dyngerous, 'yn't it? trustin' the Press? Their right 'ands never knows wot their left 'ands is writin'. [To **THE PRESS**] 'Yn't that true, speakin' as a man?

PRESS
Mr. Lemmy, even the Press is capable of gratitude.

LEMMY
Is it? I should ha' thought it was too important for a little thing like that. [To **LORD WILLIAM**] But ye're quite right; we couldn't do wivaht the Press—there wouldn't be no distress, no coffin, no revolution— 'cos nobody'd know nuffin' abaht it. Why! There wouldn't be no life at all on Earf in these dyes, wivaht the Press! It's them wot says: "Let there be Light—an' there is Light."

LORD WILLIAM
Umm! That's rather a new thought to me.

[Writes on his cuff.

LEMMY
But abaht Muvver, I'll tell yer 'ow we can arrynge. You send 'er the ten bob a week wivaht syin' anyfink, an' she'll fink it comes from Gawd or the Gover'ment yer cawn't tell one from t'other in Befnal Green.

LORD WILLIAM
All right; we'll' do that.

LEMMY
Will yer reely? I'd like to shyke yer 'and.

[**LORD WILLIAM** puts out his hand, which **LEMMY** grasps.

PRESS [Writing]
"The heartbeat of humanity was in that grasp between the son of toil and the son of leisure."

LEMMY [Already ashamed of his emotion]
'Ere, 'arf a mo'! Which is which? Daon't forget I'm aht o' wori; Lord William, if that's 'is nyme, is workin 'ard at 'is Anti-Sweats! Wish I could get a job like vat—jist suit me!

LORD WILLIAM
That hits hard, Mr. Lemmy.

LEMMY
Daon't worry! Yer cawn't 'elp bein' born in the purple!

LORD WILLIAM
Ah! Tell me, what would you do in my place?

LEMMY
Why—as the nobleman said in 'is well-known wy: "Sit in me Club winder an' watch it ryne on the dam people!" That's if I was a average nobleman! If I was a bit more noble, I might be tempted to come the kind'earted on twenty thou' a year. Some prefers yachts, or ryce 'orses. But philanthropy on the 'ole is syfer, in these dyes.

LORD WILLIAM
So you think one takes to it as a sort of insurance, Mr. Lemmy? Is that quite fair?

LEMMY
Well, we've all got a weakness towards bein' kind, somewhere abaht us. But the moment wealf comes in, we 'yn't wot I call single-'earted. If yer went into the foundytions of your wealf—would yer feel like 'avin' any? It all comes from uvver people's 'ard, unpleasant lybour—it's all built on Muvver as yer might sy. An' if yer daon't get rid o' some of it in bein' kind—yer daon't feel syfe nor comfy.

LORD WILLIAM [Twisting his moustache]
Your philosophy is very pessimistic.

LEMMY
Well, I calls meself an optimist; I sees the worst of everyfink. Never disappynted, can afford to 'ave me smile under the blackest sky. When deaf is squeezin' of me windpipe, I shall 'ave a laugh in it! Fact is, if yer've 'ad to do wiv gas an' water pipes, yer can fyce anyfing. [The distant Marseillaise blares up] 'Ark at the revolution!

LORD WILLIAM [Rather desperately]
I know—hunger and all the rest of it! And here am I, a rich man, and don't know what the deuce to do.

LEMMY

Well, I'll tell yer. Throw yer cellars open, an' while the populyce is gettin' drunk, sell all yer 'ave an' go an' live in Ireland; they've got the millennium chronic over there.

[**LORD WILLIAM** utters a short, vexed laugh, and begins to walk about.

That's speakin' as a practical man. Speakin' as a synt "Bruvvers, all I 'ave is yours. To-morrer I'm goin' dahn to the Lybour Exchynge to git put on the wytin' list, syme as you!"

LORD WILLIAM
But, d—it, man, there we should be, all together! Would that help?

LEMMY
Nao; but it'd syve a lot o' blood.

[**LORD WILLIAM** stops abruptly, and looks first at **LEMMY**, then at the cooler, still cohered with the Chinese mat.

LEMMY
Yer thought the Englishman could be taught to shed blood wiv syfety. Not 'im! Once yer git 'im into an 'abit, yer cawn't git 'im out of it agyne. 'E'll go on sheddin' blood mechanical—Conservative by nyture. An' 'e won't myke nuffin' o' yours. Not even the Press wiv 'is 'oneyed words'll sty 'is 'and.

LORD WILLIAM
And what do you suggest we could have done, to avoid trouble?

LEMMY [Warming to his theme]
I'll tell yer. If all you wealfy nobs wiv kepitel 'ad come it kind from the start after the war yer'd never 'a been 'earin' the Marseillaisy naow. Lord! 'Ow you did talk abaht Unity and a noo spirit in the Country. Noo spirit! Why, soon as ever there was no dynger from outside, yer stawted to myke it inside, wiv an iron 'and. Naow, you've been in the war an' it's given yer a feelin' 'eart; but most of the nobs wiv kepitel was too old or too important to fight. They weren't born agyne. So naow that bad times is come, we're 'owlin' for their blood.

LORD WILLIAM
I quite agree; I quite agree. I've often said much the same thing.

LEMMY
Voice cryin' in the wilderness—I daon't sy we was yngels—there was faults on bofe sides. [He looks at **THE PRESS**] The Press could ha' helped yer a lot. Shall I tell yer wot the Press did? "It's vital," said the Press, "that the country should be united, or it will never recover." Nao strikes, nao 'omen nature, nao nuffink. Kepitel an' Lybour like the Siamese twins. And, fust dispute that come along, the Press orfs wiv its coat an' goes at it bald'eaded. An' wot abaht since? Sich a riot o' nymes called, in Press—and Pawlyement. Unpatriotic an' outrygeous demands o' lybour. Blood-suckin' tyranny o' Kepitel; thieves an' dawgs an 'owlin Jackybines—gents throwin' books at each other; all the resources of edjucytion exhausted! If I'd bin Prime Minister I'd 'ave 'ad the Press's gas cut 'orf at the meter. Puffect liberty, of course, nao Censorship; just sy wot yer like—an' never be 'eard of no more.

[Turning suddenly to **THE PRESS**, who has been scribbling in pace with this harangue, and now has developed a touch of writer's cramp.

LEMMY
Why! 'Is 'end's out o' breath! Fink o' vet!

LORD WILLIAM
Great tribute to your eloquence, Mr. Lemmy!

[A sudden stir of applause and scraping of chairs is heard; the meeting is evidently breaking up. **LADY WILLIAM** comes in, followed by **MRS LEMMY** with her trousers, and **LITTLE AIDA**. **LEMMY** stares fixedly at this sudden, radiant apparition. His gaze becomes as that of a rabbit regarding a snake. And suddenly he puts up his hand and wipes his brow.

[**LADY WILLIAM**, going to the table, lifts one end of the Chinese mat, and looks at **LEMMY.** Then she turns to **LORD WILLIAM**.

LADY WILLIAM
Bill!

LEMMY [To his mother—in a hoarse whisper]
She calls 'im Bill. 'Ow! 'Yn't she IT?

LADY WILLIAM [Apart]
Have you—spoken to him?

[**LORD WILLIAM** shakes his head.

Not? What have you been saying, then?

LORD WILLIAM
Nothing, he's talked all the time.

LADY WILLIAM [Very low]
What a little caution!

LORD WILLIAM
Steady, old girl! He's got his eye on you!

[**LADY WILLIAM** looks at **LEMMY**, whose eyes are still fixed on her.

LADY WILLIAM [With resolution]
Well, I'm going to tackle him.

[She moves towards **LEMMY**, who again wipes his brow, and wrings out his hand.

MRS LEMMY

Don't 'ee du that, Bob. Yu must forgive'im, Ma'am; it's 'is admiration. 'E was always one for the ladies, and he'm not used to seein' so much of 'em.

LADY WILLIAM
Don't you think you owe us an explanation?

MRS LEMMY
Speak up, Bob.

[But **LEMMY** only shifts his feet.]

My gudeness! 'E've a-lost 'is tongue. I never knu that 'appen to 'e before.

LORD WILLIAM [Trying to break the embarrassment]
No ill-feeling, you know, Lemmy.

[But **LEMMY** still only rolls his eyes.]

LADY WILLIAM
Don't you think it was rather—inconsiderate of you?

LEMMY
Muvver, tyke me aht, I'm feelin' fynte!

[Spurts of the Marseillaise and the mutter of the crowd have been coming nearer; and suddenly a knocking is heard. **POULDER** and **JAMES** appear between the pillars.

POULDER
The populace, me Lord!

LADY WILLIAM
What!

LORD WILLIAM
Where've you put 'em, Poulder?

POULDER
They've put theirselves in the portico, me Lord.

LORD WILLIAM [Suddenly wiping his brow]
Phew! I say, this is awful, Nell! Two speeches in one evening. Nothing else for it, I suppose. Open the window, Poulder!

POULDER [Crossing to the window]
We are prepared for any sacrifice, me Lord.

[He opens the window.

PRESS [Writing furiously]
"Lady William stood like a statue at bay."

LORD WILLIAM
Got one of those lozenges on you, Nell?

[But **LADY WILLIAM** has almost nothing on her.

LEMMY [Producing a paper from his pocket]
'Ave one o' my gum drops?

[He passes it to **LORD WILLIAM**.

LORD WILLIAM [Unable to refuse, takes a large, flat gum drop from the paper, and looks at it in embarrassment.]
Ah! thanks! Thanks awfully!

[**LEMMY** turns to **LITTLE AIDA**, and puts a gum drop in her mouth. A burst of murmurs from the **CROWD**.

JAMES [Towering above the wine cooler]
If they get saucy, me Lord, I can always give 'em their own back.

LORD WILLIAM
Steady, James; steady!

[He puts the gum drop absently in his mouth, and turns up to the open window.

VOICE [Outside]
'Ere they are—the bally plutocrats.

[Voices in chorus: "Bread! Bread!"

LORD WILLIAM
Poulder, go and tell the chef to send out anything there is in the house—nicely, as if it came from nowhere in particular.

POULDER
Very good, me Lord. [Sotto voce] Any wine? If I might suggest—German—'ock?

LORD WILLIAM
What you like.

POULDER
Very good, me Lord.

[He goes.

LORD WILLIAM

I say, dash it, Nell, my teeth are stuck!

[He works his finger in his mouth.

LADY WILLIAM
Take it out, darling.

LORD WILLIAM [Taking out the gum drop and looking at it]
What the deuce did I put it in for?

PRESS ['Writing]
"With inimitable coolness Lord William prepared to address the crowd."

[Voices in chorea: "Bread! Bread!"

LORD WILLIAM
Stand by to prompt, old girl. Now for it. This ghastly gum drop!

[**LORD WILLIAM** takes it from his agitated hand, and flips it through the window.

VOICE
Dahn with the aristo—[Chokes.]

LADY WILLIAM
Oh! Bill—oh! It's gone into a mouth!

LORD WILLIAM
Good God!

VOICE
Wet's this? Throwin' things? Mind aht, or we'll smash yer winders!

[As the voices in chorus chant: "Bread! Bread!" **LITTLE ANNE**, night-gowned, darts in from the hall. She is followed by **MISS STOKES**. They stand listening.

LORD WILLIAM [To the **CROWD**]
My friends, you've come to the wrong shop. There's nobody in London more sympathetic with you. [The **CROWD** laughs hoarsely.] [Whispering] Look out, old girl; they can see your shoulders. [**LORD WILLIAM** moves back a step.] If I were a speaker, I could make you feel—

VOICE
Look at his white weskit! Blood-suckers—fattened on the people!

[**JAMES** dives his hand at the wine cooler.

LORD WILLIAM
I've always said the Government ought to take immediate steps—

VOICE
To shoot us dahn.

LORD WILLIAM
Not a bit. To relieve the—er—

LADY WILLIAM [Prompting]
Distress.

LADY WILLIAM
Distress, and ensure—er—ensure

LADY WILLIAM [Prompting]
Quiet.

LORD WILLIAM [To her]
No, no. To ensure—ensure—

LITTLE ANNE [Agonized]
Oh, Daddy!

VOICE
'E wants to syve 'is dirty great 'ouse.

LORD WILLIAM [Roused]
D—if I do!

[Rude and hoarse laughter from the **CROWD**.

JAMES [With fury]
Me Lord, let me blow 'em to glory!

[He raises the cooler and advances towards the window.

LORD WILLIAM [Turning sharply on him]
Drop it, James; drop it!

PRESS [Jumping]
No, no; don't drop it!

[**JAMES** retires crestfallen to the table, where he replaces the cooler.

LORD WILLIAM [Catching hold of his bit]
Look here, I must have fought alongside some of you fellows in the war. Weren't we jolly well like brothers?

VOICE
Not so much bloomin' "Kamerad"; hand over yer 'Ouse.

LORD WILLIAM
I was born with this beastly great house, and money, and goodness knows what other entanglements—a wife and family—

VOICE
Born with a wife and family!

[Jeers and laughter.

LORD WILLIAM
I feel we're all in the same boat, and I want to pull my weight. If you can show me the way, I'll take it fast enough.

A DEEP VOICE
Step dahn then, an' we'll step up.

ANOTHER VOICE
'Ear, 'Ear!

[A fierce little cheer.

LORD WILLIAM [To **LADY WILLIAM**—in despair]
By George! I can't get in anywhere!

LADY WILLIAM [Calmly]
Then shut the window, Bill.

LEMMY [Who has been moving towards them slowly]
Lemme sy a word to 'em.

[All stare at him. **LEMMY** approaches the window, followed by **LITTLE AIDA**. **POULDER** re-enters with the three other **FOOTMEN**.

LEMMY [At the window]
Cheerio! Cockies!

[The silence of surprise falls on the **CROWD**.

LEMMY
I'm one of yer. Gas an' water I am. Got more grievances an' out of employment than any of yer. I want to see their blood flow, syme as you.

PRESS [writing]
"Born orator—ready cockney wit—saves situation."

LEMMY

Wot I sy is: Dahn wiv the country, dahn wiv everyfing. Begin agyne from the foundytions. [Nodding his head back at the room] But we've got to keep one or two o' these 'ere under glawss, to show our future generytions. An' this one is 'armless. His pipes is sahnd, 'is 'eart is good; 'is 'ead is not strong. Is 'ouse will myke a charmin' palace o' varieties where our children can come an' see 'ow they did it in the good old dyes. Yer never see rich waxworks as 'is butler and 'is four conscientious khaki footmen. Why—wot dyer think 'e 'as 'em for—fear they might be out o'-works like you an' me. Nao! Keep this one; 'e's a Flower. 'Arf a mo'! I'll show yer my Muvver. Come 'ere, old lydy; and bring yer trahsers. [**MRS LEMMY** comes forward to the window] Tell abaht yer speech to the meetin'.

MRS LEMMY [Bridling]
Oh dear! Well, I cam' in with me trousers, an' they putt me up on the pedestory at once, so I tole 'em. [Holding up the trousers] "I putt in the button'oles, I stretches the flies; I lines the crutch; I putt on this bindin', I presses the seams—Tuppence three farthin's a pair."

[A groan from the **CROWD**,

LEMMY [Showing her off]
Seventy-seven! Wot's 'er income? Twelve bob a week; seven from the Gover'ment an' five from the sweat of 'er brow. Look at 'er! 'Yn't she a tight old dear to keep it goin'! No workus for 'er, nao fear! The gryve rather!

[Murmurs from the **CROWD**, at whom **MRS LEMMY** is blandly smiling.

You cawn't git below 'er—impossible! She's the foundytions of the country—an' rocky 'yn't the word for 'em. Worked 'ard all 'er life, brought up a family and buried 'em on it. Twelve bob a week, an' given when 'er fingers goes, which is very near. Well, naow, this torf 'ere comes to me an' says: "I'd like to do somefin' for yer muvver. 'Ow's ten bob a week?" 'e says. Naobody arst 'im—quite on 'is own. That's the sort 'e is. [Sinking his voice confidentially] Sorft. You bring yer muvvers 'ere, 'e'll do the syme for them. I giv yer the 'int.

VOICE [From the **CROWD**]
What's 'is nyme?

LEMMY
They calls 'im Bill.

VOICE
Bill What?

LITTLE ANNE
Dromondy.

LADY WILLIAM
Anne!

LEMMY
Dromedary 'is nyme is.

VOICE [From the **CROWD**]
Three cheers for Bill Dromedary.

LEMMY
I sy, there's veal an' 'am, an' pork wine at the back for them as wants it; I 'eard the word passed. An' look 'ere, if yer want a flag for the revolution, tyke muvver's trahsers an' tie 'em to the corfin. Yer cawn't 'ave no more inspirin' banner. Ketch! [He throws the trousers out] Give Bill a double-barrel fast, to show there's no ill-feelin'. Ip, 'ip!

[The **CROWD** cheers, then slowly passes away, singing at a hoarse version of the Marseillaise, till all that is heard is a faint murmuring and a distant barrel-organ playing the same tune.

PRESS [Writing]
"And far up in the clear summer air the larks were singing."

LORD WILLIAM [Passing his heard over his hair, and blinking his eyes]
James! Ready?

JAMES
Me Lord!

LITTLE ANNE
Daddy!

LADY WILLIAM [Taking his arm]
Bill! It's all right, old man—all right!

LORD WILLIAM [Blinking]
Those infernal larks! Thought we were on the Somme again! Ah! Mr. Lemmy, [Still rather dreamy] no end obliged to you; you're so decent. Now, why did you want to blow us up before dinner?

LEMMY
Blow yer up? [Passing his hand over his hair in travesty] "Is it a dream? Then wykin' would be pyne."

MRS LEMMY
Bo-ob! Not so saucy, my boy!

LEMMY
Blow yet up? Wot abaht it?

LADY WILLIAM [Indicating the bomb]
This, Mr. Lemmy!

[**LEMMY** looks at it, and his eyes roll and goggle.

LORD WILLIAM
Come, all's forgiven! But why did you?

LEMMY

Orl right! I'm goin' to tyke it awy; it'd a-been a bit ork'ard for me. I'll want it to-mower.

LORD WILLIAM

What! To leave somewhere else?

LEMMY

'Yus, of course!

LORD WILLIAM

No, no; dash it! Tell us what's it filled with?

LEMMY

Filled wiv? Nuffin'. Wot did yet expect? Toof-pahder? It's got a bit o' my lead soldered on to it. That's why it's 'eavy!

LORD WILLIAM

But what is it?

LEMMY

Wot is it? [His eyes are fearfully fixed on **LADY WILLIAM**] I fought everybody knew 'em.

LADY WILLIAM

Mr. Lemmy, you must clear this up, please.

LEMMY [To **LORD WILLIAM**, With his eyes still held on **LADY WILLIAM**—mysteriously]
Wiv lydies present? 'Adn't I better tell the Press?

LORD WILLIAM

All right; tell someone—anyone!

[**LEMMY** goes down to **THE PRESS**, who is reading over his last note. Everyone watches and listens with the utmost discretion, while he whispers into the ear of **THE PRESS**; who shakes his head violently.

PRESS

No, no; it's too horrible. It destroys my whole—

LEMMY

Well, I tell yer it is.

[Whispers again violently.

PRESS

No, no; I can't have it. All my article! All my article! It can't be—no—

LEMMY

I never see sick an obstinate thick-head! Yer 'yn't worvy of yet tryde.

[He whispers still more violently and makes cabalistic signs.

[**LADY WILLIAM** lifts the bomb from the cooler into the sight of all. **LORD WILLIAM**, seeing it for the first time in full light, bends double in silent laughter, and whispers to his wife. **LADY WILLIAM** drops the bomb and gives way too. Hearing the sound, **LEMMY** turns, and his goggling eyes pan them all in review. **LORD** and **LADY WILLIAM** in fits of laughter, **LITTLE ANNE** stamping her feet, for **MISS STOKES**, red, but composed, has her hands placed firmly over her pupil's eyes and ears; **LITTLE AIDA** smiling brilliantly, **MRS LEMMY** blandly in sympathy, neither knowing why; the **FOUR FOOTMAN** in a row, smothering little explosions. **POULDER**, extremely grave and red, **THE PRESS** perfectly haggard, gnawing at his nails.

LEMMY [Turning to **THE PRESS**]
Blimy! It amooses 'em, all but the genteel ones. Cheer oh! Press! Yer can always myke somefin' out o' nufun'? It's not the fust thing as 'as existed in yer imaginytion only.

PRESS
No, d—it; I'll keep it a bomb!

LEMMY [Soothingly]
Ah! Keep the sensytion. Wot's the troof compared wiv that? Come on, Muvver! Come on, Little Aida! Time we was goin' dahn to 'Earf.

[He goes up to the table, and still skidding a little at **LADY WILLIAM**, takes the late bomb from the cooler, placing it under his arm.

MRS LEMMY
Gude naight, sir; gude naight, ma'am; thank yu for my cup o' tea, an' all yore kindness.

[She shakes hands with **LORD** and **LADY WILLIAM**, drops the curtsey of her youth before **MR POULDER**, and goes out followed by **LITTLE AIDA**, who is looking back at **LITTLE ANNE**.

LEMMY [Turning suddenly]
Aoh! An' jist one frog! Next time yer build an 'ouse, daon't forget—it's the foundytions as bears the wyte.

[With a wink that gives way, to a last fascinated look at **LADY WILLIAM**, he passes out. All gaze after them, except **THE PRESS**, who is tragically consulting his spiflicated notes.

LITTLE ANNE [Breaking away from **MISS STOKES** and rushing forward]
Oh! Mum! what was it?

CURTAIN

John Galsworthy, eldest son of John Galsworthy (1817-1904), a solicitor and company director of Old Jewry, London, and Blanche Bailey (1835-1915), daughter of Charles Bartleet, a needlemaker in Redditch. His father's ancestors originated in Wembury, near Plymouth in England, and Galsworthy, for whom family origins were of significant importance, maintained a close connection with Devon. His more immediate family were considerably wealthy and well established in the shipping industry, and owned a fine estate in Kingston-upon-Thames called Parkfield, where Galsworthy was born on the 14th August 1867. At the age of nine he began education at Saugeen, a Bournemouth preparatory school, before starting at Harrow school in 1881 where he remained until 1886, distinguishing himself as an athlete.

His education at Harrow being successful enough to gain him entrance to Oxford, he began at New College to read law and gained a second-class degree with honours in 1889. Following Lincoln's Inn he was called to the bar in 1890. Despite this recognition he realised that he was not keen to actually begin practising law and so he resolved instead to look after the family's shipping business while specialising himself in Marine Law. This decision saw him take to the seas to destinations such as Vancouver, Island and South AFrica, though it was at the age of twenty-five on one particular journey to Australia, motivated by an (unfulfilled) intention to meet Robert Louis Stevenson on Samoa that he would being to realise fully his literary interests: though he was not considering becoming a writer at this time, his enjoyment of literature was enough to encourage an attempt at meeting a great writer and eventually enabled one of the most significant encounters of his life. He made the journey with his friend Edward Sanderson and, though he missed Stevenson, he met Joseph Conrad, a fellow future author famed for his novels which were often nautically themed. At the time Conrad was the first mate of the sailing-ship Torrens moored in the harbour of Adelaide, Australia; still very much focused on his ship-borne career, he was yet to begin his writing in earnest.

Indeed, though neither knew at the time, both Conrad and Galsworthy were at similar junctures in their lives, their time spent as sea acting as a transitional period during which each found their literary calling. It is perhaps owning to this unknown common ground that they became close friends. During his time on the Torrens Galsworthy recorded several details, offering a frank and valuable characterisation of Conrad while also illuminating his own experiences as a student of Marine Law.

> "I supposed to be studying navigation for the Admiralty Bar, would every day work
> out the position of the ship with the captain. On one side of the saloon table we
> would sit and check our observations with those of Conrad, who from the other side
> of the table would look at us a little quizzically."

On his return to England and the cessation of his nautical voyaging, Galsworthy began an affair with the wife of his first cousin, Major Arthur John Galsworthy. Ada Nemesis Pearson Cooper (1864-1956), the daughter of Emanuel Copper, an obstetrician from Norwich, remained married to the Major for ten years and the affair remained secret for its duration. In order to conceal the affair they took considerable pains to avoid suspicion. One such tactic was to stay in a secluded farmhouse called Wingstone in the village on Manaton on Dartmoor, in Devon. In Galsworthy's decision to choose Devon as the location for their clandestine rendezvous we see evidence of Galsworthy's affection for the place of his father's origin. It was only when, in 1905, she divorced the Major that their affair became known following their marriage on 23rd September of that year.

Galsworthy now took to writing sometime after having met Conrad and his career began in earnest when, in 1897, his first work, From the Four Winds, a volume of short stories, was published under the pseudonym John Sinjohn. He succeeded this in 1898 with Jocelyn, his first novel, and then his second in 1900, Villa Rubein. In 1901 he published a second volume of short stories, A Man of Devon, which was the last of his work to be published under pseudonym. The first of his work to be published under his own name was The Island Pharisees in 1904, a novel of social observation, seasoned with flashes of satire and propaganda. His decision to write under his own name is arguably owing to the recent death of his father, either as a mark of respect to his name or because now he was able to publish freely without incurring the possibility of paternal disappointment at his choice of career. It also marked a shift in his professionalism; he had hitherto published with small, independent publishers, but The Island Pharisees was published by Heinemann, a far more established House and one with whom he remained for the duration of his writing career.

He arguably cemented his position and maturity as a writer when, in 1906, he saw the publication of both his first major play, The Silver Box, and the novel The Man of Property. Each was published to considerable critical acclaim, and to achieve both in such a short space of time was impressive. the Silver Box concerns the imbalance in the justice system with regards to criminals of differing class by contrasting the treatment of a poor thief and a rich thief, both of whom stole silver cigarette cases but for very different reasons. The complexity of individual experience when not dealt with in public is highlighted and questioned in a bravely critical manner; despite the clear issues it raises with class and privilege, the final night was attended by the Price and Princess of Wales. The Man of Property was the first novel in the famous The Forsyte Saga, a trilogy of novels with an 'interlude' between each one, written between 1906 and 1921. Dealing with the questions of status, class and materialism, The Man of Property introduces us to the Forsyte family, particularly Soames Forsyte, who is acutely aware of his status as 'new money' and equally keen to assert himself as a wealthy man. Jealous of his wife and desperate to own things in order to confirm his wealth to those observing him, he engineers a plan to keep his wife from her friends which backfires spectacularly when, instead of cutting her off, all Soames achieves is enabling her to have an affair. This drives Soames to terrible actions with terrible consequences, which Galsworthy depicts with confidence.

Very typically Edwardian, the novel focuses on conflict between property and art, and to a certain degree much of its emotional power is drawn from Galsworthy's own life, particularly his affair with Ada. Their rendezvous in the countryside of Devon mirror the manner in which Forsyte seeks to relocate his wife and; though theirs was a much healthier relationship, there are clear similarities. By examining the fragile nature of the class system and those moving within it Galsworthy offered an important perspective on the relationships between material wealth, personal happiness and obsession, and the manner in which these change over time. His contemporaries widely regarded the publication of this novel as marking the end of Victorianism. His friend Conrad praised it as "indubitably a piece of art" and, though the notoriously risqué D.H. Lawrence lamented the novel's timidity in the face of sexuality and sensuality, he considered it potentially "a very great novel, a very great satire".

Though he continued to write both plays and novels, it was his work as a playwright for which he was most celebrated by his contemporaries. Indeed, his next novel, The Country House, seems uncharacteristically unfocused, its satirical view of those belonging to the country set comparatively unremarkable and weakly characterised, while at times the tone of satire becomes one of ironic detachment. In 1909 he published Fraternity, an exploration of of the various connections between urban society and the social classes therein, though its representation of lower-class Londoners is utterly unconvincing and ill-informed. Remaining with the subject of the landed gentry and the society surrounding it, in 1915 he published The Freelands, which does not stray far from conservative discussions of capitalism, the rural economy and their interrelationship.

His drama, however, featured a convincingly muted realism, directed at a relatively small, educated and politically-aware audience. His social agenda is prevalent here too, and is represented in a simple and static manner producing arresting instances of high drama. This talent for creating moments of captivating theatre is complimented by an instinctual sense of balance enabling his narratives to vacillate between their emotional high- and low-points, ultimately reaching conclusive equilibrium. This is particularly evident in one of his most popular plays, Strife, published in 1909 and examining the antagonists in a strike at a Cornish tin mine. In this, and in 1910's Justice, he approaches his subject with sympathy, irony and balance, which establishes a position of narrative authority while garnering the audiences trust that he is representing his characters and their motives justly. Justice condemns the use of solitary confinement in prisons, a reformist agenda which caught the liberality of his contemporary audiences along with the home secretary, Winston Churchill. Despite he was careful to disassociate himself with politics and professed himself apolitical, he and his work were nevertheless aligned with the views of the Liberal establishment. He spent much of the duration of the First World War working in a field hospital in France as an orderly having been passed over for military service.

Despite the popularity and brilliance of his work, it was only in 1920 that he had his first true commercial success with The Skin Game, a melodrama dealing with ethics, property and class. The play was adapted by Alfred Hitchcock in 1931. Galsworthy, meanwhile, had turned down a knighthood in 1918, considering his work not sufficient to be made a knight of the realm. He did, however, accept the Belgian Palmes d'Or in the following year. In 1920 he published the second novel in the Forsyte Saga, In Chancery, in which he resumes many of the themes of the first novel, focusing on the marital disharmony between Soames Forsyte and his wife. Katherine Mansfield considered it "a fascinating, brilliant book" in her review in The Atheneum. Then, in 1921, he was elected as the PEN International Literary Club's first president. The concluding novel to The Forsyte Saga, To Let was published in 1921 with a kind of peace being found between Forsyte and his now-ex wife, though he is left contemplating his losses and his greed. More ironic treatment of class confusions followed in Loyalties, bringing with it more popular success which lasted until 1926 and Escape, the last of his popular plays. Though he enjoyed popular success it was inconsistent and relatively small. His Collected Plays was published in 1929.

Over the course of time the appreciation of his work has gradually shifted from his plays to his novels, and particularly the detail and intricacy of his chronicle of English social difference, tension and pretension in The Forsyte Saga. Its success encouraged Galsworthy to revisit Soames Forsyte in a second trilogy, A Modern Comedy, which follows Soames's obsessive love of his daughter Fleur. In its three volumes, The White Monkey (1924), The Silver Spoon (1936) and Swan Song (1928) he examines the English commercial upper-middle class and its ideologies, its instinct to possess as its only way of distinguishing itself manifested in the poisonous materialism of Soames. Interestingly, this emergent social class which he so vehemently criticises is the very class from which he emerged. He witnessed first-hand its insularity, its chauvinism, its restrictive and oppressive morality, its stubborn imperialism and its materialism, and it is this experience which enables him to write so comfortably about it. Swan Song is widely considered among the best of Galsworthy's writing for the depth of its exploration of society and its heightened emotional subtlety. In 1929 he was appointed to the Order of Merit, despite having turned down a knighthood earlier. He spent his last years writing a third trilogy, End of the Chapter, beginning in 1931 with Maid in Waiting, Flowering Wilderness in 1932 and concluding with Over The River in 1933. These are significantly less coherent works and are indicative of his deteriorating health. Indeed, in 1932 he was awarded the Nobel Prize, though he was too ill to attend the ceremony.

Throughout the course of his career he received honorary degrees from the universities of St Andrews (1922), Manchester (1927), Dublin (1929), Cambridge (1930), Sheffield (1930), Oxford (1931), and Princeton (1931). In 1926 New College, Oxford, elected him as an honourary fellow. In photographs he is portrayed as handsome, fastidiously dressed and dignified. He was unusually compassionate and this saw him involved in several charitable and humane causes throughout the course of his life, including penal reforms, attacks on theatrical censorship and campaigning for animal rights. Though he spent the majority of the final seven years of his life at his home in Bury, West Sussex, it was at his home in Hampstead, London, that he died of a brain tumour on 31st January, 1933, six weeks after having been too ill to attend the ceremony in honour of his receiving the Nobel Prize. According to demands made in his will he was cremated and his ashes scattered over the South Downs from an aeroplane. Also in his will was his wish to leave cottages to several of his astonished tenants. He is memorialised in Highgate 'New' Cemetery and in the cloisters of New College, Oxford, where he was an honourary fellow.

John Galsworthy – A Concise Bibliography

From the Four Winds, 1897 (as John Sinjohn)
Jocelyn, 1898 (as John Sinjohn)
Villa Rubein, 1900 (as John Sinjohn)
A Man of Devon, 1901 (as John Sinjohn)
The Island Pharisees, 1904
The Silver Box, 1906 (his first play)
The Man of Property, 1906 – First book of The Forsyte Saga (1922)
The Country House, 1907
A Commentary, 1908
Fraternity, 1909
A Justification for the Censorship of Plays, 1909
Strife, 1909
Fraternity, 1909
Joy, 1909
Justice, 1910
A Motley, 1910
The Spirit of Punishment, 1910
Horses in Mines, 1910
The Patrician, 1911
The Little Dream, 1911
The Pigeon, 1912
The Eldest Son, 1912
Quality, 1912
Moods, Songs, and Doggerels, 1912
For Love of Beasts, 1912
The Inn of Tranquillity, 1912
The Dark Flower, 1913
The Fugitive, 1913
The Mob, 1914
The Freelands, 1915
The Little Man, 1915

A Bit o' Love, 1915
A Sheaf, 1916
The Apple Tree, 1916
The Foundations, 1917
Beyond, 1917
Five Tales, 1918
Indian Summer of a Forsyte, 1918 – First interlude of The Forsyte Saga
Saint's Progress, 1919
Addresses in America, 1912
In Chancery, 1920 – Second book of The Forsyte Saga
Awakening, 1920 – Second interlude of The Forsyte Saga
The Skin Game, 1920
To Let, 1921 – Third book of The Forsyte Saga
A Family Man, 1922
The Little Man, 1922
Loyalties, 1922
Windows, 1922
Captures, 1923
Abracadabra, 1924
The Forest, 1924
Old English, 1924
The White Monkey, 1924 – First book of A Modern Comedy (1929)
The Show, 1925
Escape, 1926
The Silver Spoon, 1926 – Second book of A Modern Comedy
Verses New and Old, 1926
Castles in Spain, 1927
A Silent Wooing, 1927 – First Interlude of A Modern Comedy
Passers By, 1927 – Second Interlude of A Modern Comedy
Swan Song, 1928 – Third book of A Modern Comedy
The Manaton Edition, 1923–26 (collection, 30 vols.)
Exiled, 1929
The Roof, 1929
On Forsyte 'Change, 1930
Two Essays on Conrad, 1930
Soames and the Flag, 1930
The Creation of Character in Literature, 1931 (The Romanes Lecture for 1931).
Maid in Waiting, 1931 – First book of End of the Chapter (1934)
Forty Poems, 1932
Flowering Wilderness, 1932 – Second book of End of the Chapter
Autobiographical Letters of Galsworthy: A Correspondence with Frank Harris, 1933
One More River (originally Over the River), 1933 – Third book of End of the Chapter
The Grove Edition, 1927–34 (collection, 27 Vols.)
Collected Poems, 1934
Punch and Go, 1935
The Life and Letters, 1935
The Winter Garden, 1935
Forsytes, Pendyces and Others, 1935

Selected Short Stories, 1935
Glimpses and Reflections, 1937
Galsworthy's Letters to Leon Lion, 1968
Letters from John Galsworthy 1900–1932, 1970
Caravan the assembled tales of John Galsworthy, New York Charles Scribner's Sons 1925